Living at Summerhill

LIVING AT SUMMERHILL

In Photographs by Herb Snitzer

ORIGINALLY PUBLISHED AS *Summerhill: A Loving World*

COLLIER BOOKS

TO all children
> with a hope that they are given
> the opportunity, which is rightfully
> theirs, to live and love

TO A. S. Neill and Victor Nielsen,
> two men who have made me see and
> feel more fully and deeply

This Book is Dedicated

O glad, exulting, culminating song!
A vigor more than earth's is in thy notes . . .
A reborn race appears—a perfect world, all joy!
Women and men in wisdom, innocence and health—all joy!
Riotous laughing bacchanals fill'd with joy!
War, sorrow, suffering gone—the rank earth purged—nothing
   but joy left!
The ocean fill'd with joy—the atmosphere all joy!
Joy! joy in freedom, worship, love! joy in the ecstasy of life!
Enough to merely be! enough to breathe!
Joy! joy! all over joy!

Walt Whitman

Contents

1. Summerhill

SUMMERHILL SCHOOL is located in the town of Leiston, county of Suffolk, one hundred miles northeast of London. The Headmaster is A. S. Neill, a man now eighty years old. In this book you will meet A. S. Neill, and read his words on what the school means and how he conceived and nurtures it. The children and all the others connected with the school you will meet in much the same way. I have taped conversations and discussions with the children, the staff, and Ena, Neill's wife.

A few years ago I read a book by A. S. Neill, in which he spoke of the school, its forty-year history, and what he had accomplished in that time. Never before was I so moved by a man's writing on children. I was determined to meet and speak with this man, and so I flew to England in 1961.

Below are some thoughts I put down on paper after returning to America:

> Summerhill—a school for children where a philosophy of love is lived. Where at any given moment fifty children are experiencing what it is to know themselves. A school where there are no laws of morality or religion. Where children are free to grow into adulthood without the psychological patterns most of us experience. Children who can express themselves without fear of beatings or unfair accusations. Where mental and physical conditioning are left to the child. Where coercive methods of compulsive education do not exist. At Summerhill the children regulate themselves.

1

My first meeting with A. S. Neill took place on a cold November morning. I was waiting in the staff room, a room filled with books and beat-up furniture, with a big table in the center, surrounded by a few chairs. The door opened, and a man in well worn corduroy trousers, a sweater pulled over a washed and faded wool shirt, big black shoes, and silver-gray hair, walked over to me and simply said, "Hello, I'm Neill." We talked about why I came to Summerhill. The meeting was brief, since he had to return to his classes. I asked him if I could wander about, to which he replied, "You're free to do as you wish," and walked out.

During my stay I had the opportunity to take a long walk with Neill, and we spoke of many things. Especially the bomb, and the feeling that one day it will be used. "How can men who are so basically antilife not use it eventually? They are our leaders, but they are as sick and psychologically pathetic as the man who has fears of walking down a dark street." These words were spoken by Neill with deep compassion and feeling.

We talked about the financial problems of Summerhill and how hard it is to keep the school going, for only through Neill's books and lecture tours is Summerhill able to make up the deficit from which it continually suffers. Very little money comes in from contributions or from former students (yet in this area Neill is content, for he feels that when children leave Summerhill, they should leave it completely, and when this happens he is sure that the process has worked.) "If you need to keep returning to your home, to a former school, there is something lacking within yourself. The greatest compliment I can receive is when I see former students come up for end-of-term parties and just walk right by me with a nod and an hello, and then join in with the party. When they linger or hang around, whether it be with me or the staff, I know that somewhere something failed."

We talked of the amount of property damage at Summerhill. It seemed that fifteen new children had arrived, and they were experiencing Neill's freedom. The thrill of breaking things without physical punishment was getting the better of them. It was left to the older students to straighten this out, but this takes time—years, not days. A child repressed and full of hate cannot love in a matter of days, and so the pattern continues, and so do the bills. I saw children treat each other kindly and unselfishly, ruthlessly and horribly; yet I knew that in time, under the watchful eyes of Neill and the staff,

the ruthless will no longer feel the necessity to let out on others what they feel about themselves. In time they will know themselves and will be able to see others with a love that makes living a beautiful experience.

I said goodbye to Neill and Ena on a dark evening and, wondering whether I would ever see them again, I walked alone to the deserted station platform from which a train would take me back to London, back to a system I now more fully understood. As the train approached, the door of the station burst open, and out came about fifteen Summerhillians to say goodbye, and to shake my hand or grab at my arm. They clowned and laughed, and as the train picked up speed, they raced down the platform. A split second later there was darkness. I stopped waving and sat down, crying with feelings I had never known before. I closed my eyes and thought of Neill, a man of seventy-eight sitting in his study in Summerhill, looking forward to another day which will bring fifty children closer to themselves.

3

Through good fortune I was able to return to Summerhill in September, 1962, to live and to photograph a way of life that can be explained in one word—love. I stayed in Summerhill until the Christmas holidays. I leave the rest to you—to see and to feel, freely, what happened.

Leiston is a small town with a population of 4,250. The principal industries are a machine-and-tool factory and a safety-wear plant. There is a small canning factory as well, but for the most part Leiston would become quite a desolate place to live if the machine factory closed. This one plant employs most of the people living there. The houses are almost all made of the same red brick, dulled through the years. There is a post office at the town square, a cinema, one hotel, a few pubs (one being the Engineers Arms, where I spent many pleasant evenings by the fire), one traffic-light intersection, the usual number of necessary shops: grocers, hardware, shoe repair, cleaners, and so on. There are four schools and five churches. The *Leiston Observer* is published once a week. You don't feel that Leiston changes much from year to year. The only evident innovation is that all the brick tile roofs and chimneys have now been mounted by television antennae. That possibly makes the lives of these people a bit more comfortable. Although not poor (the average weekly income is about thirty-three dollars), the people seem to be resigned to their existence. They are very polite, but never spontaneous. Everybody, including the children, looks old. The town is quiet and lonely after the sun sets. The pubs close at 10:30 p.m. (11:00 on weekends).

The townspeople are more or less indifferent toward Neill. For the most part they think he is a slightly balmy man in what he advocates for children; few of them understand his ideas to begin with, but they maturely concede that, if parents want to send their children to this school, it is their responsibility, and something not to be interfered with. The Summerhill kids have very little contact with the boys and girls of the town. They feel the town kids are just silly children, interested in things they themselves have outgrown years ago. Every so often, the town kids come to Summerhill to play the boys in English football (soccer) and here the differences can be poignantly seen and felt. The Summerhill boys are more interested in having fun and playing than in winning. They would like to win—there is no getting away from this—but they are interested in having a good time as well, whereas the town kids have only one thing in mind—to score, and beat Summerhill. The looks on their faces are something to see. The determination becomes almost fanatical, and you realize at once that the game is not

4

fun at all, but a battle, which unfortunately may be carried throughout their lives. The Summerhill boys want no part of this type of competition, for they intuitively realize that it has very little meaning. Where the joy of doing something disappears, the children of Summerhill leave it alone.

The national school examinations, called the GCE's (General Certificates of Education), are taken by Summerhill students who wish to go on to university level. In most schools these examinations are uppermost in the minds of the students, and many of them study for years to pass the tests. At Summerhill classes are optional. You can attend or you can stay away. If you attend, you are expected to know the work, and to do the work, for there are no examinations. The theory is: you attend; therefore you want to learn. And the boys and girls do learn. It is not a rare thing for Summerhill children to start classes when they are twelve or thirteen, and in the remaining three years accomplish what other schools spend seven or eight years driving into their pupils. The classic example in Summerhill was a lad of fifteen who decided he wanted to go on to the university, but was told he had to pass his GCE's first. In his remaining year and a half he studied and worked very hard, for the university was something he *wanted*. He passed the tests, and is today an Assistant Professor of History at Manchester.

2. A. S. Neill

Hıs words will speak for him, and my photographs will say what I want to say. I believe he is one of the great men of this world. He has given his love to children so that their own lives will be full and happy ones. What he has done in these past forty-one years and what he continues to do today are difficult to express in one book after three short months of living in Summerhill.

His influence is everywhere in Summerhill—the kindness, softness, and warmth that everyone feels. His weekly discussions with the children and staff on life and the living of it show a man who truly practices what he believes. The one thing that is most important in understanding Neill and all of Summerhill is that he is far more interested in the child now, than in what the child will become in later years. "The end product will take care of itself. If the child has the love and freedom to function as a human being equal to his parents, teachers, or any adult, he will have the chance to live a happy life."

◈

Questions I am frequently asked are: "How do I justify Summerhill at all? What's the difference between Summerhill and other schools?" Well, there are various answers. I think the best answer is that I did the logical thing. I don't think I did anything special. Freud discovered that the unconscious is the important thing— that the emotions are more important than the intellect. There are schools based on the intellect alone. I started a school where I thought the emotions should come first. Thirty years ago I might

6

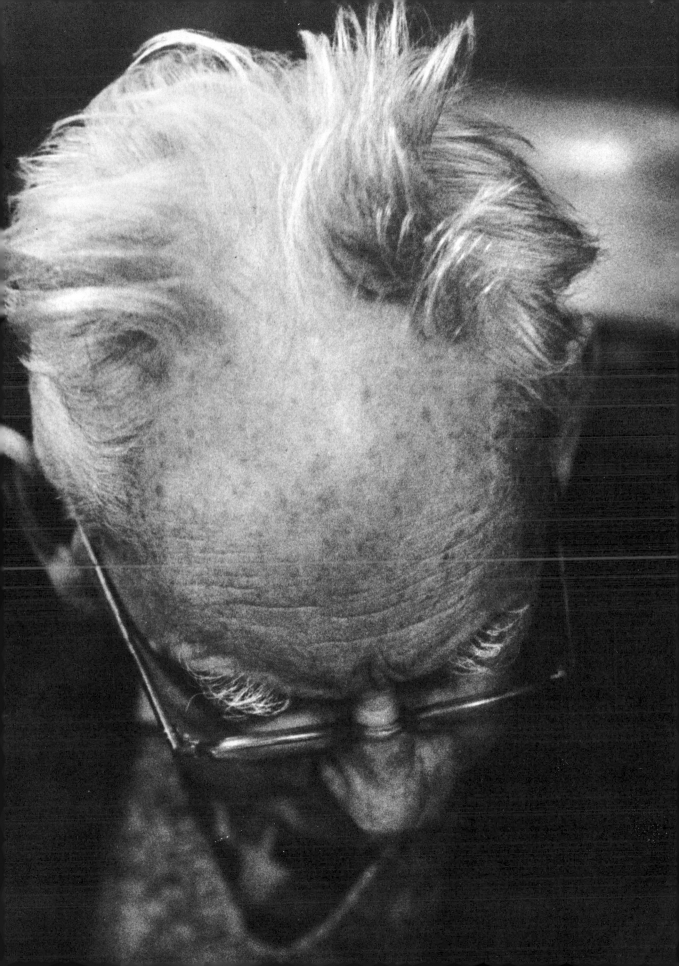

have given a different answer, but today Summerhill signifies that the world is very, very sick, and we don't have to convince ourselves of that. All we have to do is look in the newspapers. Now, many things have been tried. Religion has been tried and never lived up to. Morality has been tried. Politics has been tried. Nobody ever tried the one thing I tried. You see, in the patriarchal society that we live in, we are conditioned in our cradles. Our characters are molded the moment we are born, either by timetable feeding or by stupid ideas about being clean, and so every kid in the world, you and I included, the whole lot of us, have been symbolically castrated in our cradle. That's why society waits for one gentleman named K to press a button, and we don't do anything about it. Oh, some try. I tried in my own humble way, but after two nights in prison I gave it up. We're all waiting for our fathers: Father Kennedy, Father Macmillan, Father Khrushchev. We want them to make up our minds for us. Mind you, to be fair, I must ask, "Are the older and former students of Summerhill doing any more than anyone else?" That's the idea behind Summerhill—that freedom must be tried, and it has never really been tried. I always distinguish between freedom and license. It's quite simple. Freedom is doing what you want, as long as it doesn't interfere with somebody else. Well, that's the basis of the school—putting the emotions first, for, you see, nothing of importance comes from the head. You don't fall in love by thinking about it. You don't see a pretty girl and say, "I think I'll fall in love with that girl." It is the same with religion or politics. You don't do it by thought alone. When I threw a tomato at Winston Churchill some years ago in Dundee, the district leader's daughter, who handed me the tomato, was very pretty, but then that was something else. What I want to say is that our emotions are the things that guide our lives.

I am also always asked, "Are your former pupils rebels?" That's a difficult question to answer. You see, I have a suspicion that you become a rebel when you've gone through the mill. I was brought up under strict education, and so rebelled. Homer Lane rebelled. Otto Shaw rebelled. We all rebelled against something. Now, when you're brought up in freedom as you are at Summerhill, do you rebel or not? I don't think you do. I don't think it is necessary. To rebel is one thing; to challenge is another. I can't imagine any old pupils having a color complex or being anti-Semitic, or bringing up children with a fear of God, or with a sex complex. I can't imagine they do, and I'm content to believe this.

8

❧§❧

People have told me that I have a father complex because I rebelled against the system, and so started a school of my own. These same people don't seem to be able to tell me why it is that, out of a family of eight brothers and sisters, I was the only one to go this way. This they have no answer for, and, I might add, I don't either.

❧§❧

Children grow up today in a world filled with lies and fear. "Johnny, if that is Mrs. Smith at the door, tell her I'm not home." Or Johnny breaks a cup at the dinner table and he is hit, yet the next night his father does the same thing, and his mother smiles. What will a child think? My dog Biscuit is a nice dog, a quiet dog, but if I chained him up for a fortnight, he would start snapping and biting at people. We chain our children. I just wonder how much influence is exercised by a mother who has a child yet to be born within her—a child she really doesn't want. How much of her stiffness is passed on to the child, so that when the child is finally born he or she is deformed? I mean mentally deformed. It is something I think about all the time.

❧§❧

Children are innately honest, and they expect you to be the same way. It is one great thing about childhood. They are open and honest, and if allowed to experience freedom will remain this way all their lives without the shutting up of their feelings toward others. They won't be afraid to love someone.

❧§❧

Children should find things out for themselves. They shouldn't be told that Beethoven is better than Ellington. I think parents intimidate children too much by suggesting that they like one thing better than another thing. A child shouldn't have to take on the tastes and ideas of grown-ups. Our school is run on self-government, and the children are the ones that govern. We have law-breakers here as in any system, but they keep the laws better.

❧§❧

We don't tell children what to do; we only teach them technique. If a boy came to me with a piece of copper, and said, "What

Children are honest because they don't know any better. Old people are honest because they do.

9

should I make?" I would say, "I have no idea; that's for you to decide." But if he came to me and asked me how to join two pieces of copper, I would say, "I'll show you." Only children that come from disciplined schools ask what they should paint or what they should make. If a child of sixteen, who had been here since he or she was five, came to me and asked me something like that, I would be shocked, and I've never been shocked that way in forty-one years.

✤

I have a great objection to a teacher who comes along and sees a child playing with mud, and uses this as a chance to talk about coast erosion, or some nonsense like that. Play should be completely separated from learning. I object strongly to systems that use play to make children learn something. Play to me means no strings attached to it at all.

✤

In the main, people who have been through Summerhill have a certain charity toward people, and a certain balance with life. Put it in a negative way: I can't imagine anyone here becoming a fascist. The children have too wide a view of humanity for that. From the beginning they understand tolerance.

✤

If we had these horror comics from America, I think I would chuck them out. I wouldn't have such things here. I don't think it's fair for a small child to be faced with all that perversity and sickness that we call humor, made by sick men—mind you—perverted men. I'd kick them out, just as I wouldn't have one of the Gestapo on my staff. There are certain things you protect yourself against.

✤

Living should be for itself—not for money, not for success, not for Cadillacs. I've often said that I would rather have a contented busman than a neurotic B.A. as an old pupil. Now, nobody can be happy all the time. You aren't happy when you have a toothache or when your best girl runs away with someone else. By happiness I mean a sort of feeling that life is good in the main, that you are enjoying life without hating and struggling with other people to get somewhere. I think this struggle to get somewhere is awful. No system can claim that it is the cat's whiskers. I would never claim that all my old pupils are all balanced in every way. How could I?

The only hope for us is to let children alone without indoctrinating them in any way, and the tide is running against us. Communism is based on indoctrination. The whole of Americanism is a subtle indoctrination all the way. I don't know why America and Russia quarrel so much. They are alike in many ways, especially when it comes to teaching methods for children.

❧

No one can be entirely free. You have to obey laws. You must drive on the left side of the road. You have to obey the policeman. What I mean by freedom is inner freedom. If a child doesn't want to learn mathematics it is no one else's business but the child's, but if a child wants to play a trumpet while others are asleep, then it is everybody's business. We try at Summerhill to distinguish between the two. . . . In a good home the children and the parents have equal rights. In a bad home either the children have all the rights or the parents have all the rights.

❧

The popular press idea of free children is that they break windows all day long. Freedom is nothing of the kind. Freedom in Summerhill is living your own life without outside interference. When children come to freedom for the first time at the age of twelve or thirteen, they don't know what it is, and it takes time for them to realize that you can't do exactly what you like at Summerhill.

❧

I'm not trying to produce any kind of person here. I'm only trying to let people be themselves without outside interference. No one should dare say they are trying to produce a certain kind of person. Nobody is good enough to try to tell a child how to live or what to do. I believe that if they can govern themselves and are free from fear, free from compulsion to develop a sincerity and a character of their own, the rest will take care of itself. Freedom gives you a tremendous amount of sincerity. I can't imagine any old pupil standing up on television and saying that something washes whiter than something else, because he would know it is a lie.

❧

We are all liars. Now, it isn't a terrible thing if you tell a lie. We all do. What is terrible is when you live a lie. There are people who hate their bosses, hate their jobs, smile at customers when they don't want to smile. When a child lies he is often imitating his parents or

his teachers or other adults. . . . If a child breaks something and he is afraid of his mother or his father, he lies and says he didn't do it—the cat did it. This sort of lying you can eliminate by having parents and teachers who do not make children afraid of them.

❧

Summerhillians do find it difficult to adjust to the outside world in the beginning—not so much the ones who come from London where they have their own group, but if you get pupils from Birmingham or Glasgow, they complain that they find it difficult to meet people who feel the same way they do. But they can adapt themselves far better and far faster than any other people I know. I think that free people will have a greater sense of what is around them. One of my oldest pupils, the second one I ever had, spent a whole year in a motor factory putting nuts onto bolts, and he hated it, but he stuck with it because he wanted to be an engineer, which he is today in Scotland, and a very good one at that.

❧

The criticism that I underplay the intellectual for the emotional part of a child is partly true. I had to emphasize the emotional aspect, and I hold that if your emotions are free your intellect will look after itself. That's why I think you'll find that people who do want to learn will learn quickly. Our children pass the national examinations after studying for two years, while other schools take five or six years to prepare for the same examinations. They are emotionally free, and can concentrate on what they are doing. I'm not against learning. I'm against making learning the only thing in schools. Every educational journal is filled with learning—nothing about living. After all, I went through the university myself, and I'm supposed to be an educated man. I don't think I am, though.

❧

I was never influenced by the big educators. I never read Dewey or anyone else. I came to education through psychology—through Freud and Reich. I had a long analysis myself, and thought, as so many people did, that psychoanalysis would change life for the better. There would be no more crime, no more unhappiness—but this is nonsense. I don't object to analysis. I just think it is limited to those who have the time and the money to lie on a couch. There is no hope for humanity in that. That's not the way. The only other way is to let children be free so that they won't need analysis.

13

☙§❧

I'm not a Freudian. I was influenced very much by Freud. I was also influenced very much by Homer Lane, an American I call a genius with children. I was influenced by Wilhelm Reich, but much later. He had no effect on my work, but he was brilliant, and the greatest psychologist since Freud. You never really know who is influencing you. I'm called a pioneer, but what is a pioneer? I'm a mixture of Freud, Reich, Lane, Wells, and Shaw and everybody else I've ever read. There is nobody who does anything original. All I've done is apply the knowledge of men conscious of the true meaning of education. Most schools ignore the fact that we should look at children as free beings who have the consciousness to choose what they want.

☙§❧

I suspect that there are neurotic people who have gone through our school. I always say that the successes are due to the school and the failures are due to the parents. This might be so, at that. No system of education can entirely correct a bad home. If you were a boy who had a stepmother who hated you, and you hated her, and every time you came back from a holiday you acted like a little savage hating everybody, destroying things, just how much could we do? You can take the boy away from home, but then he'll feel different because other boys have homes. . . .

☙§❧

People always ask how former pupils get on. By getting on, I presume they mean, are they making money? Do they have a car? Are they keeping up with the Joneses, and all that? Why people are so concerned with this I'll never really know. It is enough for me to get a child of ten who is filled with hate and fear and in five years to see him go away a happy and wonderful person. That is enough. I have no worries about that person in later years. So, three are university lecturers, one is a barber, two own pubs, one is a potter, some are engineers, a few are musicians, two are actresses, one is a ballet dancer, two are nationally known painters, one is a top poster illustrator in London, but so what? What is getting on? . . . So far we have produced no geniuses. One book review said Summerhill children are not ambitious. It is possibly true. They're not ambitious to make money, but they are ambitious at their own jobs, and that's enough. They are not ambitious to own a big house or a Cadillac to impress people. They go far beyond that. And

another thing they go far beyond is snobbery. . . . Free children
have a scope that others do not possess.

At present I can't imagine a system based on what I have tried
to do, because there aren't enough parents who would agree with
this way. Today in England and America there are millions of kids
in schools. I have fifty-two. It's only a tiny minority who would send
their children to a school like this. Forty years ago there were no
schools that practiced what we practice, yet today many schools
are somewhat free. That's good. Maybe in the future there will be
more. I hope so. The children of the future will be happier for it.
So will the world.

3. Ena Neill

Iᴛ ɪs difficult to say anything new about Summerhill. Neill has written about it, and said all that I might have to say. We agree about the basic and important issues in Summerhill.

The original idea of Summerhill was to have a school for normal children, but because of Neill's insights and psychological skill, he has been asked, over the years, to take problem children of all kinds. So, I guess Summerhill has become erroneously known in some places as a school for problem children. We are trying now to take better-balanced children. They too have their problems, which are solved to some extent by living in a community which is without fear and run by self-government.

Educating a child at Summerhill is a long-range project, and parents need to have great faith, not only in the school, but in their children. They must, of course, wholeheartedly believe in our system.

When Neill is no longer able to take an active part in the running of the school, he considers that I will be fit and able to do so. Although I do not have his brilliant insight into the child's mind, I do have plenty of sound common sense. I also love children enough to want them to grow up in the only way I believe to be the right way—the "Summerhill way." I have lived and worked in the community for twenty-three years, learning from Neill all the time.

I shall never change Summerhill, its self-government and the approval of the child's right to live his own life in the way he feels is best fitted for him.

We have a great many American children now, and they are

different from the English children. Many of them, though not all, have a very material approach to life. They also have an artificial veneer of sophistication which is a little frightening. But this is soon lost when they are left alone to just be themselves. They all have a great zest for living both mentally and physically, and they also bring in some new and original ideas which often help to solve certain community problems. For a time some of them also add to community problems.

My position in the school is not altogether an enviable one, for I get most of the hate and only some of the love that goes to most parents. I must act *in loco parentis* for all the American children. Their parents leave it to my discretion as to what their children shall have or not have. If and when I do have to say "No," I get all of the resentment that they feel—and in many cases cannot show— toward their own parents. In Summerhill they show these feelings without any reserve, and this can make life difficult. I try to meet this with patience and understanding, and with a good sense of humor these matters are usually quickly solved.

I have no words of wisdom about the life or about Summerhill. I know only that what I have gathered over the years from living in a community such as Summerhill and from working closely with Neill, I try to apply right back in the daily life of Summerhill in dealing with the children. To me that is the important thing.

4. The Staff

IN MOST living structures there is always one man or a few men who lead the way. Some dominate to the point where individuality and freedom are suppressed. Such a thing does not exist in Summerhill. It is difficult at times to tell the staff from the pupils, for the staff live the same sort of life. There are, of course, rules by which the children govern themselves that do not apply to the staff (bedtime laws, for example). In Summerhill staff members are equal to the children and nothing more. No staff member would think of telling a child to attend lessons, or would ask a child to do something the staff member would not do himself. The children recognize the differences between themselves and the staff members, but they are the differences of age and knowledge, not those based in fear. A child told me, after seeing a staff member twisting, "My God, to think that is my French teacher!" In time that child will emotionally understand that his French teacher is a human being as well.

Being a staff member is an all-day occupation. It is a living experience, and the staff is on call constantly. Bedtime is at ten-fifteen, but if a child has a pressing problem and turns to a staff member rather than to one of the older students, that staff member will sit with the child for hours, if necessary. The rooms of the staff are constantly filled with children listening to Bach or Armstrong, or talking between themselves or among groups on subjects that pre-occupy every child or teenager. What they say, they say freely, and they are given the respect that is rightfully theirs.

One of the continuous problems that Summerhill has faced in its forty-one years is how to maintain a high-level staff, who believe in freedom, can teach, and also have a love and respect for the community of children. Outside of its being an exhausting job, the pay is low—thirty pounds a month, with room, board, and laundry. This is equivalent to about ninety American dollars, and although the average income in England is a great deal lower than that in America, thirty pounds is not nearly enough.

A staff member in Summerhill does not worry about the money —at least not for a few years. If pay were higher, perhaps some of the really fine teachers would remain longer. Money has always been a pressing problem at Summerhill. The school is in the red continuously, despite the many lecture fees Neill earns throughout England, Scotland, and the Continent. There is a need for a science teacher, but what science teacher would be willing to devote his entire life to a school that can pay him only thirty pounds a month, when he knows that another school or industry will pay him much more? The chemistry lab was well equipped, but it lay idle, and so has been converted into a photographic darkroom.

The staff consists of seven men and women, not counting Neill, who concentrates mainly on private lessons (called PL's) with the children and a growing correspondence. He does continue to teach geometry and algebra. There are an art teacher; a teacher-house-mother for the children of kindergarten age; a German teacher who also instructs in needlecraft, sewing, and knitting; and a teacher of ancient history and English. There are also a teacher for pottery and woodwork; another who teaches French and Spanish and is also involved with the digging of potatoes, feeding the many chickens, picking apples, and making the fires; and finally a teacher for history, English, geography, elementary reading and writing, as well as workshop.

28

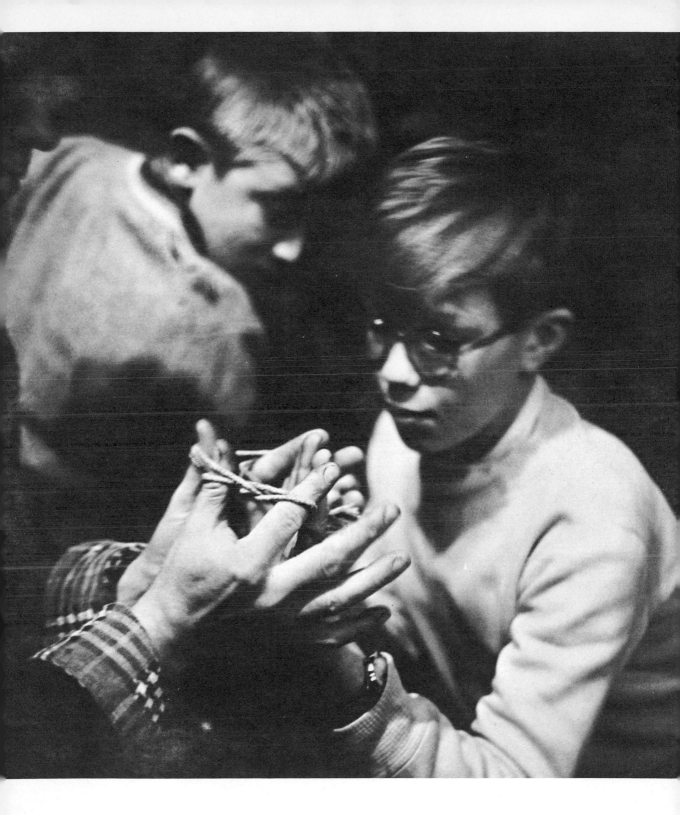

29

5. Tuesday-Evening Discussions

EVERY TUESDAY EVENING, Neill leads a discussion to which pretty nearly everyone comes and contributes. Psychology, Good and Evil, Self-Government, Swearing, and Lessons are only a few of the many things discussed. The talks usually begin with Neill making opening remarks, posing questions, and stimulating the kids and the staff to talk freely and spontaneously. Most of the time what comes out is wonderful and exciting for everyone.

Most of Neill's remarks are in the form of questions rather than dogmatic statements. He is more interested in having the kids reach their own conclusions than in giving them his theories formulated from eighty years of living. "What's the sense of telling someone something? You shouldn't try to change that person. You can only get him to think a bit more."

The discussions usually begin with some broad topic that eventually narrows down to the immediate life in Summerhill. The children really open up as it comes closer and closer to home. There is no hesitation on the part of the pupils to use the names of other students or staff members when they have something to say, and this is done with the purpose of helping themselves, the other person, and the school. I saw and heard both Ena and Neill taken to task by students for things they had done which were not liked by the students. In the same way I heard a staff member criticize the students, each interacting with the others. Out of this something constructive for everyone would evolve. Here was another example of children not afraid to say what they felt. They spoke openly and honestly, and what they said was respected by all present.

The discussions are not always serious. If Neill sees the opening for one of his usually "bad" jokes, he will take it, and the kids will come down on him for it. It is then you can feel the love Neill is giving, the love that is being returned by the kids—the real accomplishment of Summerhill.

Just the looks on the faces of the children were enough for me to say, "*Yes, this is real.*"

NEILL: *I'm not going to give you a lecture, for I spend enough time outside the school doing just that. I don't plan to talk much, for I want you all to join in and to speak up with what you have on your minds. I'm going to tell you a little bit about people in general as human beings. Now, you two shut up. It's tiresome being interrupted all the time. Now, being conscious means you know things. You can see things. You can talk and think. You are all conscious that I am talking now. That's part of a human being. Behind this is what psychologists call the subconscious. That is where we store things, like a cupboard—we store things we know, but don't want to remember; and behind that is a place we call the unconscious, which is a place where we shut off all the things we don't want to think about. You shove something there, and very often you lose it. For example, when I was little I knew a boy who, one night in a joking mood, said to another little boy, "I'll shoot you," and he didn't know the gun was loaded and he blew the little boy's head off. That little boy was a friend of mine. Well, anyway, afterwards the other boy forgot all about it. He buried it. He seemed to forget all about it. It was buried because it was so unpleasant that he didn't want to remember it. Now, behind all this—and this is deep stuff—is a place called the id, and that's the deep thing that makes you breathe. That's very difficult to explain. I know it's difficult, but each person here, you and I, we are all the same. We have all these things inside us. We're conscious of things, and we're unconscious of things, and now I'm going to ask you a question. I don't want to lecture all the time. Now, where does this come from? You see, if you were brought up on a desert island with nobody to speak to, you wouldn't know anything, would you? Oh, you'd know how to piss and shit, but you*

39

*wouldn't know how to talk about things. Now, where
do you get all the things you know? Brendan?*

BRENDAN: *You learn it.*

NEILL: *What?*

BRENDAN: *You learn it.*

NEILL: *Right. From whom?*

BRENDAN: *People.*

NEILL: *Right. So everybody depends on people. Who are
the first people you depend upon?*

BRENDAN: *My mother and father.*

NEILL: *So your mother and father are the first people to teach
you all sorts of things. Do they teach you well, or do
they teach you badly? Do you think fathers and
mothers are the best people to teach you things?*

BRENDAN: *They try to teach you well, but it doesn't always turn
out that way because little things might go wrong
when you're young and become bigger when you're
older, and they come back on you.*

NEILL: *Okay. The first people who train you to live are your
fathers and mothers; and if they are wise people
things will work out, and if they aren't they'll make
a mess of things. Now, all of you look into yourselves
and ask yourselves. Am I a mess or not?*

[Laughter]

*When you get older and you leave your mother and
father, why do you go to school?*

ROY: *To learn things.*

NEILL: *What sort of things?*

ROY: *Arithmetic.*

GWEN: *Geography.*

NEILL: *Why do you learn these things?*

LARRY: *It helps you later on.*

ROZ: *It helps you to know things.*

NEILL: *Good. Now we're getting to two points here. There
are two points to a person. There is what you think
with, and there is what you feel with, namely, the
head and the heart. Tell me something: Does this
school deal with the head or the heart?*

BRENDAN: *The head.*

NEILL: *Does it?*

ROY: *The head and your heart.*

NEILL: *The head and your heart. Good. Now, what do we
do with our head?*

JERRY: Math and things.

NEILL: Anything else go to the head?

ROZ: Practically everything goes to the head, Neill.

NEILL: All right, what goes to your heart? Your guts, if you like. I don't mean what you eat. Nothing? Hands up those who come from other schools. Now most other schools deal with learning in the head and they don't deal with what you feel. Emotions are what we call them. Hey, Roy, name an emotion, will you?

ROY: Panic.

NEILL: Panic? You mean fear.

JOYCE: Love.

LISA: Hate.

NEILL: Right. Are sausages an emotion?

[Laughter]

All right, you clever people. What's the connection between emotions and sausages?

LARRY: When you shit, it feels good.

[Laughter]

NEILL: All right, but more than that.

SUSIE: Hunger.

NEILL: Hunger, right. Now, you new kids: in a few short sentences I'll tell you the differences between Summerhill and other schools. In an ordinary school you have to learn things with your head. You have to obey, and do what you are told. You have to sit quiet in a classroom in most cases, and then go home at night and learn geometry, history, and other things. Summerhill is different. Somebody tell me what's the difference? Someone who has just come from America. Millie.

MILLIE: It helps you to get on with people, and in America you have to go to classes. Here you don't.

NEILL: Yes. Anyone else?

LISA: You can do what you want.

NEILL: Can you?

LISA: I mean classes. You can choose what you want to learn.

NEILL: You're free to do what you want. You're free not to think if you don't want to. But you're not free to break the laws. Right? Well then, why, if you're free, here's the question—free people are supposed to be happy people. Why, then, do we have so many people at Summerhill breaking the laws? 43

GWEN: *Because freedom is something you don't grasp right away. You go through an antisocial period.*

NEILL: *You go through an antisocial period. Now, is that natural? Must everybody be antisocial?*

MILLIE: *For a certain time, Neill.*

NEILL: *Why?*

MILLIE: *Well, when they find they are so free, they sort of go nuts, just breaking every law.*

ROY: *Well, I don't think that has to happen. I think it depends on what has happened to you in the past.*

NEILL: *Good, good. Well, this is quite an interesting discussion. Millie says that people have to go through an antisocial phase, and Roy says it's not necessary, and that it is something in your background that makes you nasty—that makes you hate.*

JOYCE: *Well, sure, Neill, but something goes wrong in practically every child. Nobody grows up perfect. There is always something. It's not only the new kids who are antisocial.*

NEILL: *Ah, you've got something there. It's not only the new kids, but it's lots of the old kids who have been here for years. Now, why are they antisocial?*

SCOTT: *Because they get used to it.*

ERNIE: *Because they don't think it's free enough here.*

ROY: *Oh, Ernie, pack it in, will you?*

NEILL: *Wait a minute. Will some antisocial person who has been here for forty years tell us why it is necessary to be this way?*

[Laughter]

ERNIE: *Because we're bored.*

NEILL: *Bored?*

ERNIE: *Yes, bored.*

NEILL: *With what?*

ERNIE: *With the school. With freedom.*

CAROLE: *That's rot. What happens is that when they go home they have to do things they don't have to do here, and so when they come back they take their hate out by being antisocial here.*

NEILL: *Well, is Carole saying that some of our homes are bloody awful, and that we don't want to go back to our homes?*

ROY: *Yeah, in my case it is.*

44 MILLIE: *Mine too.*

NEILL: *It's interesting that with other schools the kids want to go home for holidays, but here, most of you want to stay.*

JERRY: *Well, if you came from my home you wouldn't either, Neill. My mother hates me.*

NEILL: *Well, whatever is wrong at home seems to make these same people antisocial here. Okay. Hands up, those people who aren't antisocial.*

ROY: *Oh, come off it, will you? Look who has his hand up.*

NEILL: *All right. I'll ask another question and see if the same people raise their hands. Hands up, all those that are liars.*

[Laughter]

Now I'll tell you something, and this is interesting. Your behavior in Summerhill and everywhere else goes back to somewhere in your home or your first school or something like that, and if you were nasty, and you didn't like your home—your father bossed you or your mother bossed you—and you left home, you would boss somebody else. So I'm asking you a question. Is a bully a person who was bullied by his father or mother?

GWEN: *Not necessarily. It could be a boy who was bullied by other boys and girls, or other adults.*

JOYCE: *Any adult can frighten a child, can't he?*

NEILL: *Of course. Could a strict teacher frighten a child who has been brought up by a free mother and father?*

ENA: *I would think that if a child is intelligent enough— he could begin to reason things out when a strict teacher tries to bully him. The main stem would come from a nice home and understanding parents. Nearly every child I know, though, thinks the parents of other children like him better than his own parents do.*

SCOTT: *Neill, I'd like to ask you a question. Is that why brothers and sisters fight?*

NEILL: *Yes, very often. You always think a person likes someone else better than another. If you ask your mother and father, and they say they like all of you the same, this wouldn't be true, for of course they couldn't, or do they?*

SCOTT: *Well, in my family it's true.*

NEILL: *All right, now. This is interesting. When people come*   45 to Summerhill and they break things and they steal things, is it because their mothers and fathers were strict with them, or they had a little brother or sister that they hated, or is it they want to show off in front of people, or what? This is what I have wanted to say all evening. Why do people do things?

ROY: Because they have a bad conscience.

NEILL: All right. He speaks of conscience. What's a conscience, everybody? Conscience is the part inside of you that makes you feel guilty. If you steal something, you feel guilty about it, and this is an interesting thing in psychology. Sometimes crooks have such a guilty conscience they want to be caught and punished. They don't know it, of course, and they get punished by leaving their fingerprints on the safe. They make some obvious silly mistake, but it isn't such a silly mistake, is it? Conscience tells you, you've done something wrong. Where does this come from?

GWEN: From your environment.

NEILL: Yes. In other words, a boy brought up in Central Africa hasn't the same conscience as a boy brought up here in England.

CAROLE: Look, Neill, some people kill during war, and they aren't guilty about that.

NEILL: They aren't. Why?

ROY: Because the state says it is a good thing to do.

NEILL: Because the state says it is a good thing to do. It is good to kill in war. They give you medals for killing in war, and they give you the chair for killing in peacetime. All right. Why do people have a conscience about stealing?

JERRY: Because they know it's wrong.

MILLIE: Because it's against the moral standards that your father and mother gave you. Not necessarily your parents, but all the people in your life.

NEILL: Now, Myrna, suppose your father was a clever crook, which he isn't, but suppose he sent you out when you were six or seven to pretend you were blind. Would you have a bad conscience?

MYRNA: Well, it would depend if it were for a cause. If we were starving I wouldn't feel guilty.

ENA: Well, I'm damn sure that if the little ones here pinched something they wouldn't feel guilty about it at all.

46

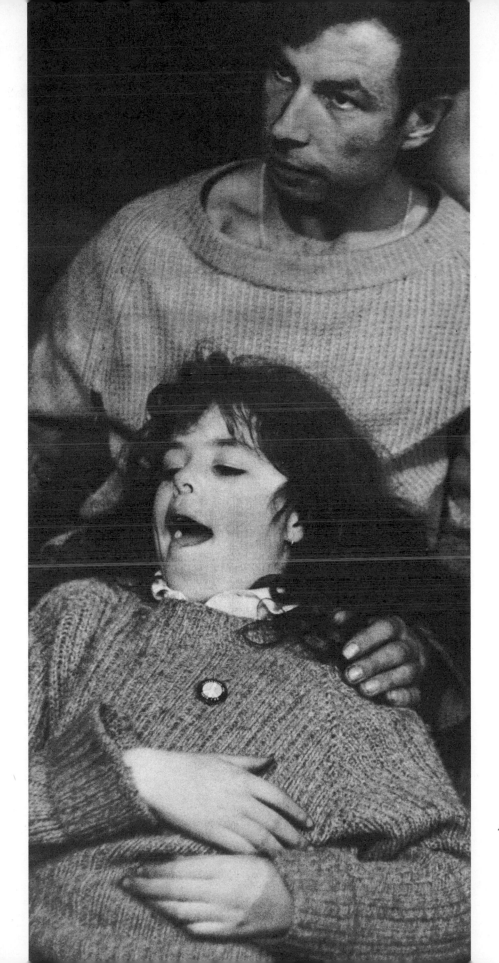

NEILL: *Tell me. How many people here are honest because of fear? How many of you would steal if you could? How many would travel from here to London without a ticket if they knew they wouldn't get caught?*

MYRNA: *Well, that's not stealing. I mean, it's stealing, but it's not really stealing. It's not the same thing as going into your office and stealing the money box.*

NEILL: *It's the same thing.*

ROY: *Well, it's the same thing, but it's different. I don't know the railroad, and besides, they won't miss it. It belongs to the government, and they take enough money off us anyway.*

NEILL: *Ah, that's very nice. What we call rationalization. It's like the man who makes out his income tax and hides a thousand quid and then says, "Well, they cheat me, so why shouldn't I cheat them?"*

JOYCE: *Look, Neill, there are two reasons why people steal. Either they want something you've got, or else they do it out of spite.*

NEILL: *All right, now. People don't steal because they want money or want what you've got. They steal because they're unhappy. No happy person ever stole. You think about that. If you're happy, you couldn't steal. If you think somebody loves you, you wouldn't steal. People who steal always think somebody doesn't love them.*

SCOTT: *Do you consider it stealing when a young child takes something?*

NEILL: *Oh, no, not at a very young age. He doesn't know what this means, but you see, in a way someone who steals is someone who has never grown up. Nobody is truly honest. There never was an honest person who lived. All right, now. I guess you can have a guilty conscience about sex as well. About shitting on the floor or pissing. In your early training someone tells you it's dirty, and you remember it. Oh, not consciously you don't, but raise your hands now. How many wash before eating? You see. Now why do you do that?*

JERRY: *Well, there are germs on your hands.*

NEILL: *Do you think about this if you find a cigarette on the ground?*

JERRY: *Well, no.*

NEILL: *No, of course you don't. Why not, now? Is it because*

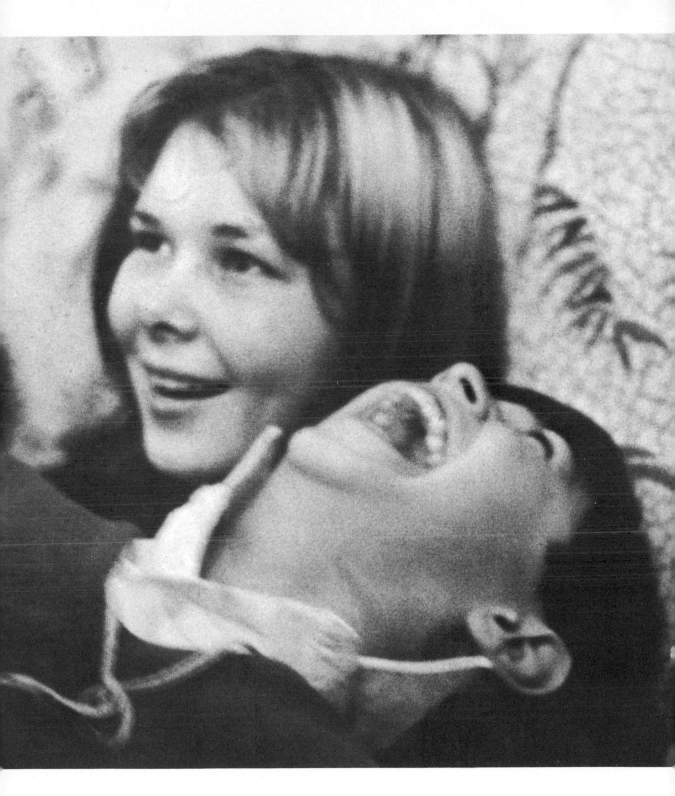

49

you haven't been told that was dirty? Because it was
something you wanted? Do you think the same thing
happens to your sex parts as well? You're told they're
dirty in many ways. You're told not to touch them,
not to ask questions about them. So what happens?

GWEN: Well, you think they aren't nice.

NEILL: That's right. Well, are they or aren't they nice?

GWEN: Well, I always thought they weren't nice, but I never
told anyone.

NEILL: Okay, and so you thought everyone else thought they
weren't nice as well.

GWEN: That's right.

NEILL: Do you see how far this can go? Do you see why some
people talk about bathroom jokes? They can't talk
about their sex parts straight away, and so do it in a
roundabout way. Now, getting back to conscience, do
you think you have a better chance of having a life
if you don't have guilty feelings about all these things?

ROY: Sure, Neill. Honestly, that's a pretty silly question.

NEILL: Is it? Would you think it silly if I told you that the
reason many of you are antisocial is because you feel
guilty about things, and this is the way it comes out?
Ah, we've spent enough time tonight. We'll have
another talk next week.

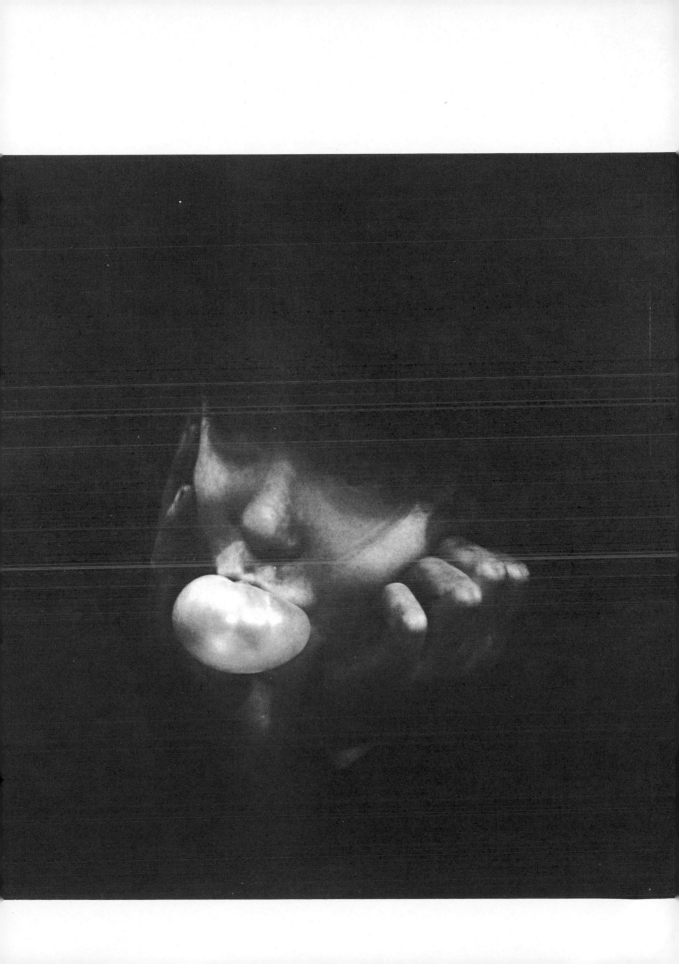

54

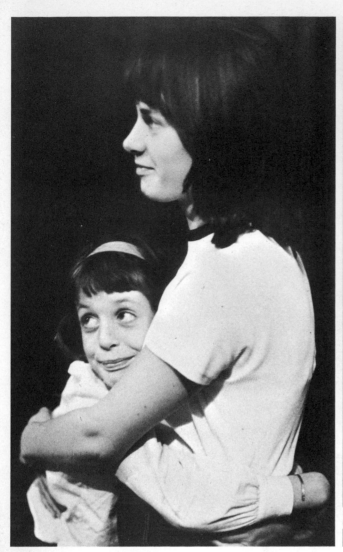

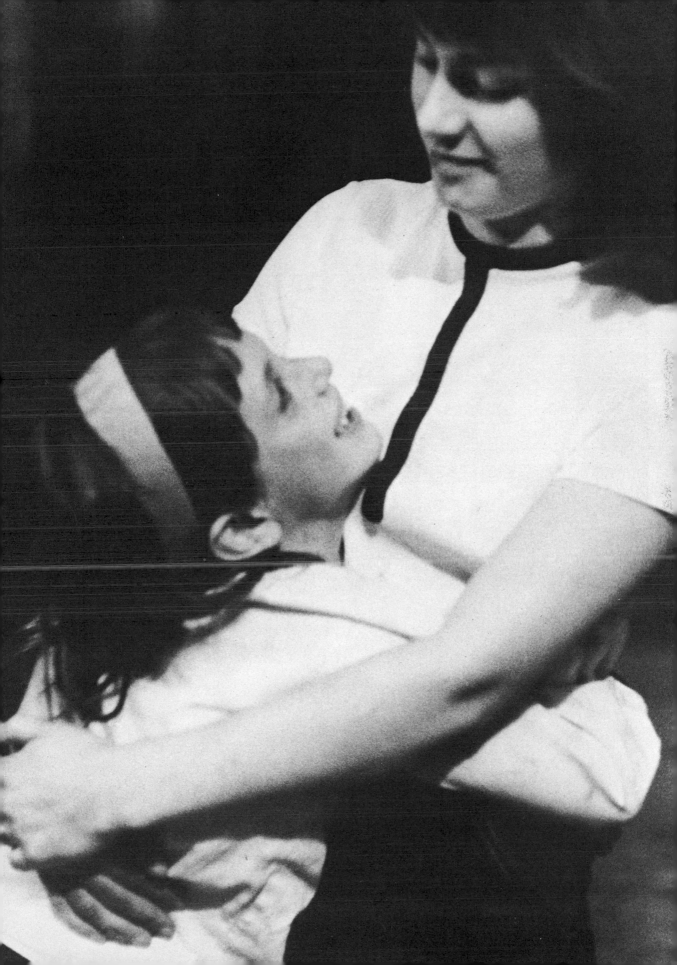

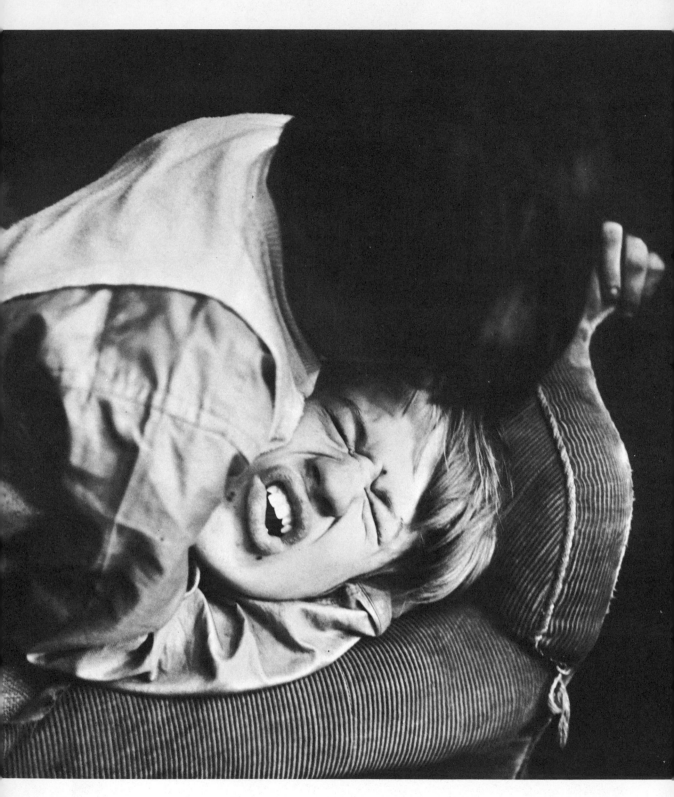

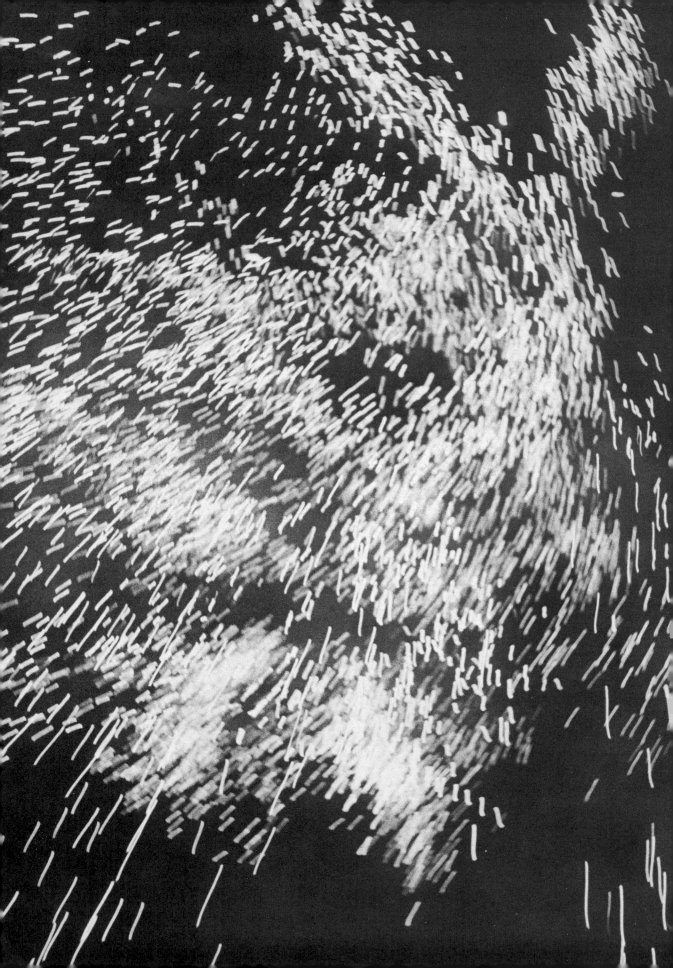

67

6. Swearing

NEILL: The discussion tonight will be about swearing. Now, I want your opinions about this. There is a lot of swearing that goes on in the school—more than usual—and I want to know why people swear. Why do they use words that lots of people don't like to hear?

SCOTT: Well, a lot of the new kids haven't been allowed to swear at home, and so they do it here.

ROY: It becomes a habit, Neill.

LARRY: Well, I think it's easier than to think up something original.

GWEN: Well, I notice that the old Summerhillians swear just as much as the new kids.

ROY: I don't swear at home, but here it's just sort of natural.

JOYCE: The trouble is, Neill, if you call someone some nice long word from the dictionary, they don't know what you mean. They miss the point.

MARTY: It's also that those long words don't have the point. I mean you swear, and it comes across.

LARRY: It just works, Neill.

CAROLE: It also can have a great deal of affection attached to it, Neill. When you call someone an old bastard, you may mean it in a very warm way.

NEILL: All right. I want you to think about this aspect of swearing. The world outside has a lot of people in it who don't like it. And most of you don't swear when you're home. I know this. So you use Summerhill to do things you wouldn't do at home. Is swearing a danger

to Summerhill? Most of your parents know that people swear here, and they don't mind, but sometimes
you get a case with a child, for example, whose uncle
or grandparents are paying the fees, and the first word
they hear is a curse word, and so they say, "Well I'm
not going to pay money to send a child to this school,"
and out the child goes. I'm asking you, is it a good
thing to keep swearing, and lose the child from
Summerhill?

ROY: *If they have that sort of background, Neill, you can
stuff them.*

NEILL: *That has nothing to do with it, Roy. Suppose your
mother and father believe in Summerhill, which we
will assume they do, and they can't afford the fees, but
your uncle Jim says he'll pay the fees, and he comes
here and he hears swearing, and he goes home and
tells your parents he isn't going to pay the fees. So
you'll be taken away, you chump.*

CAROLE: *Look, Neill, when the kids here swear, they don't
think the words they are using are dirty. The people
who come here are the ones with the dirty minds.*

ROZ: *Are you trying to have a discussion, or are you trying
to get us to stop swearing, Neill?*

NEILL: *I'm having a discussion. I can't stop you from swearing. You know that.*

ROZ: *People who come here expecting to find a bloody old
place can jolly well go back again.*

WOOD: *It's not Summerhill, Roz.*

ROY: *Look, Neill, this is our school. The visitors don't pay
to come here.*

NEILL: *Do you pay?*

ROY: *Oh, damn, Neill, you know what I mean.*

SCOTT: *Look, if a visitor comes here and sees we swear and so
keeps little Johnny away, he was looking for an excuse
anyway. He could pick on any topic, you know.*

CAROLE: *Surely, Neill, when kids come here, and they swear a
lot, it shows they have a complex about something,
and are getting it out. You start putting bans on it,
and before long they will assume these are naughty
words, which they aren't, and so all you will do is drive
it back into them.*

GWEN: *You might as well have the girls wearing dresses and
the boys wearing ties. The visitors might like that.*

71

NEILL: I'm going to bring up something else. There is such a thing as good manners. Good manners means behaving toward people so you don't offend them. You don't go into a Roman Catholic house and swear against the Holy Ghost. That's good manners. Is it good manners to shout out swear words to people who don't like them? Are you conscious enough to know when to use swear words or not? That's the question I'm asking.

ROY: The visitors come to us, Neill. We don't go to the visitors. If you go to a friend's house and she does something you don't agree with, you don't go and tell her. You would think that wrong.

SCOTT: When we go out of Summerhill, we conform to that society, and we go by their rules, and so when people come here they can jolly well conform to ours.

NEILL: I might remind you that not long ago someone in town said that the language of the Summerhill children was a danger to the nice children of Leiston.

JERRY: Neill, you should go to the cinema and hear the differences between the downtowners and the kids from Summerhill. If you think we're bad, you should listen to them.

VAN: It isn't only here that people swear. It's just that we do it openly. When I went to secondary school, we used to swear all during the break, all through lunch hour, and all through playtimes or whatever the hell they're called, behind the teacher's back. And we thought we were really something, you know, but now when I swear it expresses my feelings, and that's it.

NEILL: I'm not making it a moral question. I'm making it a financial question. Am I going to lose a pupil through swearing? That's my point.

OLLY: How long has it been since you've lost a pupil that way, Neill?

NEILL: I can remember one man who—

OLLY: One man in over forty years of teaching, Neill?

[Laughter]

NEILL: —came here after four weeks and heard things, and shoved this kid in the car and never came back. I was rather pleased in a way. I didn't give him back his fees.

[Laughter]

JERRY: How many million years ago did you say that was, Neill?

CLANCY: Let me ask you a question, Neill. Would you rather have nice kids who don't swear openly, but giggle and swear behind your back, or would you rather have free kids who swear openly and who don't think it's dirty?

ROY: Look, Neill, if you were angry at a friend, what would you say?

NEILL: Well, look, Roy, I'm an old man now, and I can control my language. I'm a gentleman, and I have a good vocabulary. I don't need to use those words.

OLLY: Neill, if a kid comes from a repressed home, surely you're happy for him to swear. Suppose a kid was from a repressed home, and he is frightened to swear, and obviously has a conscience about swearing—well, surely this is worse than for a kid to come right out with it.

NEILL: You're right about that. I'm talking about the older ones here, who seemingly can't control themselves. I feel they should have outgrown it by now.

OLLY: Then why do you use these words, Neill?

NEILL: No, not me.

OLLY: Sure you do, Neill. I've heard you. When you get annoyed sometimes you swear.

CAROLE: Ho ho, Neill, what about that?

CLANCY: Yeah, Neill, you're caught.

NEILL: I say what the bloody hell. All right, okay, you've had me.

[Laughter]

To take it another step. Filthy stories, filthy sex stories are only there because sex was repressed when you were children.

MILLIE: The reason people laugh at these so-called filthy stories, Neill, is because they are actually funny.

NEILL: You do?

MILLIE: Of course I do, when they are funny.

NEILL: Why's it funny? Because it's dirty?

MILLIE: Oh, hell, Neill. Why is anything funny, then? Why do you like dirty jokes?

NEILL: I don't like dirty jokes.

MILLIE: You've told me quite a few, you know.

NEILL: At the university—I must confess this—I was famous in about three thousand men for having the best selection, and looking back now, there is hardly one that I would keep. And the one or two that I have kept have a point.

73

CAROLE: *In the four years I've attended your lessons, you let out jokes to us every once in a while, and they've all been about lavatories. Now why?*

JERRY: *Oh, Neill, you're finished now.*

NEILL: *That's true, quite true. You see, I'm a psychologist, and I have to adapt myself—*

SCOTT: *Pack it in, Neill.*

NEILL: *—to the people who look the part. I guess all the classes you've been to have been anal neurotic. You're trying to defend your guilt by putting it onto me.*

GWEN: *Come off it, Neill.*

MARTY: *That's not good enough.*

MILLIE: *I guess this proves we are all pornographic slobs, so let's pack it in or change the subject.*

SEVERAL
VOICES: *Hear, hear!*

NEILL: *All I'm asking is that you be conscious of what you say, and control your tongues as much as you can when Aunt Mary is about. Okay, I think that's it for tonight.*

ROY: *Oh, Neill, just when we get interested, you always pack it in. What's on television?*

7. Lessons

Lessons are not compulsory. You can go, or you can stay away, but if you go, you are expected to be reasonably quiet.

The classes are held in the mornings and late afternoons. Most of the time, they are held in the lesson huts, but on really cold days they are usually transferred by the wishes of the students, and the teacher as well, either to the teacher's room or to the staff room; in the summer, they are held outdoors.

The beginning of a term usually finds most of the kids going to classes, but after about two weeks of this, the ones who aren't really interested or ready to learn drop out. These are usually the younger ones who would rather play all day.

One child who impressed me above all others was a twelve-year-old boy who didn't attend too many classes, and couldn't read very well, but whose interest in tape recorders, music, and photography was fantastic. He made photograms in the school darkroom that were as beautiful as anything I've seen. He and a few of the older boys strung telephone wires all over the school grounds, and by the end of the term had planned a hook-up between his room and four or five other rooms. He has something books could never give him, and when he leaves (even if he never attends another class) he will be a wonderful adult.

I attended only a few classes, since I was more interested in other facets of the school, but the classes I did visit were as free and as wonderful as the rest of the life in Summerhill. The children did not take on other personalities once they stepped inside the lesson huts. They were just as relaxed and just as free, and the relationship be-

78

tween "pupil" and "teacher" was one of ease and mutual respect.

The children who attended classes learned and absorbed the material at a much faster rate than I could ever recall myself or my former classmates doing. There are no examinations and no homework.

One incident I recall vividly was attending two French classes on consecutive days, the second day being a review of what was learned the day before. None of the kids had opened their French book from one day to the next, and I spent a great deal of time with them, just to see if they reviewed the work before going into the classroom for the second day. None did, yet they were able to do

79

the review easily, with everyone joining in. I was completely amazed, recalling the hours of homework and the fear within me if I went into a class "not prepared."

⋖§ Neill Teaching Algebra §⋗

(There were five children present)

NEILL: *All right, this is our first algebra class, so I'll begin by saying that in algebra we deal with letters instead of numbers. Is that clear? For example (writing on blackboard):*

$$a + \quad a = 2a$$
$$b + \quad b = 2b$$
$$3a + 6a = 9a$$

Now, how much is four people and three horses?

ROY: *It's seven living things.*

NEILL: *Oh, very clever. Now, what's the answer?*

ROY: *There isn't any, Neill. You can't add people and horses. It's the same thing as adding apples and oranges.*

SCOTT: *Hey, does anybody have an apple? I'm hungry.*

NEILL: *All right, there. Shut up. Good, good, so then since you can't add apples to oranges, you can't add an a to a b.*

CLANCY: *Hey, can we try?*

NEILL: *Oh, shut up there. All right, try this problem (writing on blackboard):*
$$4a + 9a + 6a - 3a$$

JOYCE: *Here it is, Neill—sixteen a.*

NEILL: *Right.*

ROY: *Hey, that's kind of nice and easy, isn't it?*

NEILL: *All right, here's another. See what you do with it.*
$$4a + 3a + 7a - 2a - 5a$$

ROY: *Oh, bloody hell, Neill.*

NEILL: *Come on. It isn't difficult.*

SCOTT: *Finished, Neil. The answer is seven a.*

NEILL: *Right. Try this one.*
$$5a + 6a - 2a - a$$

CLANCY: *What the hell you mean, "minus a," Neill?*

NEILL: *Minus a is minus one. You don't write "1a," you just write a. Don, can you do it? Here, I'll show you. Oh, hell, he isn't even looking.*

TOM: The answer is eight *a*.

NEILL: Here, try this one.

$$4a + 2b + 2a$$

Now why don't you add the *a* and *b*?

CLANCY: Because you said we can't.

NEILL: You idiot! I didn't say it. You reasoned it out for your-selves. Remember?

CLANCY: Oh, yeah, we did, didn't we?

ROY: I don't get it, Neill.

NEILL: I didn't think you would.

ROY: Oh, shut up, Neill.

NEILL: Now, what is the answer?

ROY: Six *a* plus two *b*.

NEILL: Good, so you can do it. Now watch this (writing on blackboard again):

$$a = 1 \quad b = 3 \quad c = 2$$

Find out what this is equal to. (Writing on black-board):

$$2a + 3b + 5c$$

CLANCY: It's sixteen, Neill.

NEILL: What did you say?

CLANCY: Sixteen.

NEILL: Anyone else?

JOYCE: Twenty-one, Neill.

ROY: You do it, Neill.

NEILL: All right, I'll have a go. Roy, tell me what is two *a*.

ROY: It's two, Neill.

NEILL: And three *b*?

ROY: Nine.

NEILL: And what's five *c*?

ROY: Ten.

NEILL: All right. Add them together and what do you get?

ROY: Twenty-one.

NEILL: All right, we'll keep the same values.

$$6a - 2b + 3c - 2a - 4c$$

TOM: Oh, that's a tough one.

NEILL: What do you have, Roy?

ROY: Stop looking at my paper.

TOM: It's *a* minus four, Neill.

NEILL: Are you sure?

TOM: Sure.

NEILL: Well, let's see. Right you are, Tom.

81

TOM: Hey, will you look at Neill and his package there. Hey, Neill, only a Scot would keep that package.

NEILL: Oh, no, Tom, I think that's a Jewish trait as well.

TOM: Hell, no, Neill. A Jew would throw it out and get another.

NEILL: You know why there are no Jews in Scotland, Roy?

ROY: Sure, what Jew in his right mind would live there anyway, Neill? Ha, ha.

NEILL: It's because the Scots drove them out.

ROY: Hey, will you listen to him. Come on, Neill, on with the algebra.

NEILL: All right, here is a new value scale:
$$a = 0 \quad b = 1 \quad c = 2$$
So, what is a plus b plus c?

ROY: Three. God, Neill, that was easy.

NEILL: All right, you smart ones, try this:
$$3a + 4b - 2c$$
You have the answer?

JOYCE: Oh, keep still, Neill, we're still doing it.

NEILL: Okay, okay. What did you get, Roy?

ROY: Eleven.

NEILL: What did you get?

JOYCE: Four.

NEILL: What did you get?

TOM: Zero.

NEILL: Zero is right. Roy, how did you get eleven?

ROY: It wasn't easy, Neill. Oh, Christ, I used the wrong scale.

CLANCY: Oh, hell, I can't get this stuff at all. Neill, are we going to have algebra all week?

NEILL: Yes, we are.

CLANCY: Well, I'll see you next week then. (He gets up and leaves.)

NEILL: All right, one more before the bell. New scale:
$$a = 0 \quad b = 0 \quad c = 10$$
$$2a - 4b + 3c$$

JOYCE: Oh, Neill, you're a bloody riot.

NEILL: Roy, last night I taught Biscuit to count apples, and he counts better than you. Isn't that something?

ROY: What the hell's the joke, Neill?

NEILL: Okay, okay, there's the bell. Get out of here, all of you.

ROY: Hey, Tom, what's the joke? Hey, Herb, do you know the joke?

83

TOM: *Did you ever see a dog count, Roy?*
ROY: *Oh, that Neill. He's always pulling my leg.*
TOM: *You're too serious sometimes, Roy.*
ROY: *Oh, shut up, Tom.*

❧ French Class ❧

WILF: *There's your book, Judy. On the table there. Right. Well, what I want to do is go over the pronunciation of the words we had yesterday, and then I'll write a paragraph on the board in French, so that we can translate it, and read it. Right. Judy, you read the first four.*
JUDY: *Le professeur, la ligne, le crayon, le pupitre.*
WILF: *Not pew, but pu. Here, watch my lips. Now try it again, and remember, push your lips forward. Good. Gwen, the next four. Okay, that was fine. Roz, you do the next four. Good, good. Scott, the next four.*
SCOTT: *Oh, I can't do it.*
WILF: *Sure you can. Try it. See, it was simple, wasn't it?*
GWEN: *Oh, Jerry has the three nicest words of the lot.*
WILF: *Which are they?*
GWEN: *"Voici," "manger," and "oui."*
WILF: *Right. Millie, the next four. Right, fine. Marty, the next four. Good. You all did very well. All right, I'm going to write a paragraph on the board and you copy it. (Goes to the blackboard.)*

La Salle de Classe
Voici la salle de classe. Voici Millie. Voici Jerry. Voici le professeur. Où est Judy? Judy est dans la salle de classe. Je vois Clancy. Voyez-vous Lou? Où est Herb? Herb est dans la salle de classe. Je vois Scott. Le professeur est dans la salle de classe. Je vois le professeur. Voyez-vous le professeur?

JUDY: *What do you want us to do, copy it?*
WILF: *Yes, and then read it.*
MILLIE: *Oh, Christ!*
WILF: *And then we're going to ask questions about it.*

MARTY: *Blimey, I can read French! How about that?*

WILF: *What does "voyez-vous" mean?*

JUDY: *"Do you see," you bloody idiot.*

LOU: *I don't know what all these words mean.*

JUDY: *Well, you should pay attention.*

LOU: *I am paying attention.*

JUDY: *Well, how come we all know the words, and you don't?*

WILF: *All right. By the time we finish, we all will know the words.*

MILLIE: *Wilf, do you pronounce the names in French the same way as you do in English?*

WILF: *Some of the names. Now, repeat after me: Où est Herb? No, no. Remember you don't pronounce the h in French. All right, Millie, would you like to translate for us?*

MILLIE: *Well, the room of the class.*

WILF: *No, you just say "the classroom."*

MILLIE: *Here is the classroom. Here is Millie. Here is Jerry. Here is the teacher. Where is Judy? Judy is in the classroom. I see Clancy. Do you see Lou? Where is Herb?*

WILF: *Right, good. Roz, you do the next ones.*

ROZ: *Herb is in the classroom. I see Scott. The professor is in the classroom.*

WILF: *Well, actually, "le professeur" is "the teacher."*

MILLIE: *Hey, Wilf is a professor.*

LOU: *Wilf is a slob.*

[Laughter]

WILF: *Thank you for those kind words. Le professeur est dans la salle de classe.*

LOU: *The slob is in the classroom.*

WILF: *Okay, the slob is in the classroom.*

ROZ: *Where is the teacher?*

WILF: *"Je vois" is "I see," and "voyez-vous" is "do you see."*

ROZ: *That's correct.*

WILF: *Thank you. Scott, would you read some of it?*

SCOTT: *Do I have to?*

WILF: *Come on now, you can read it.*

SCOTT: *Here is the classroom. Here is Millie. Here is Jerry. Here is the professor.*

WILF: *The teacher.*

SCOTT: *Okay, the teacher.*

WILF: *You can say "professor." It sounds good.*

SCOTT: *Where is Judy?*

85

JUDY: *I'm here.*

SCOTT: *I see Clancy.*

CLANCY: *Do you?*

ROZ: *Hey, I propose we throw those people out if they want to play around.*

WILF: *Okay, that was fine, Scott. What's the time?*

SCOTT: *It's five twenty-seven.*

WILF: *Let's go over them again. Actually, if you added an e to Herb it would be "grass" in French.*

MILLIE: *How come it isn't Herb? I thought you leave off the h in Spanish? Are you sure you aren't getting mixed up?*

SCOTT: *Yeah, Herb is an American, and there is no such word in French, so why wouldn't you say Herb?*

WILF: *Yes, but remember, we're speaking French.*

JUDY: *Wilf, if a French person comes up to you and asks your name, you wouldn't say "Erb," you'd say "Herb."*

ROZ: *Yeah, Wilf, what about that?*

WILF: *The Frenchman would call me "Erb."*

ROZ: *Oh, Wilf, they wouldn't.*

WILF: *Of course they wouldn't because my name isn't Herb in the first place.*

SCOTT: *Herb is a plant, isn't it?*

WILF: *Right, now get out of here, everybody. It was good today.*

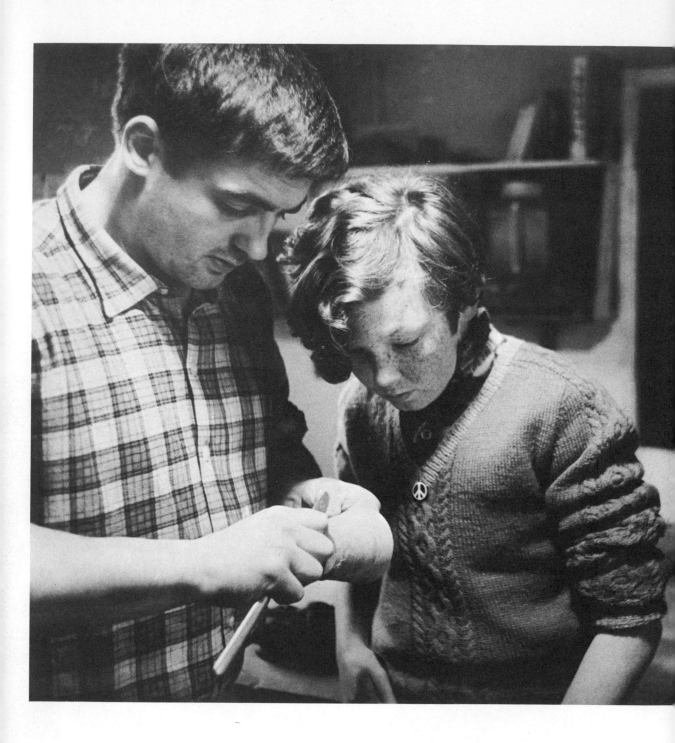

92

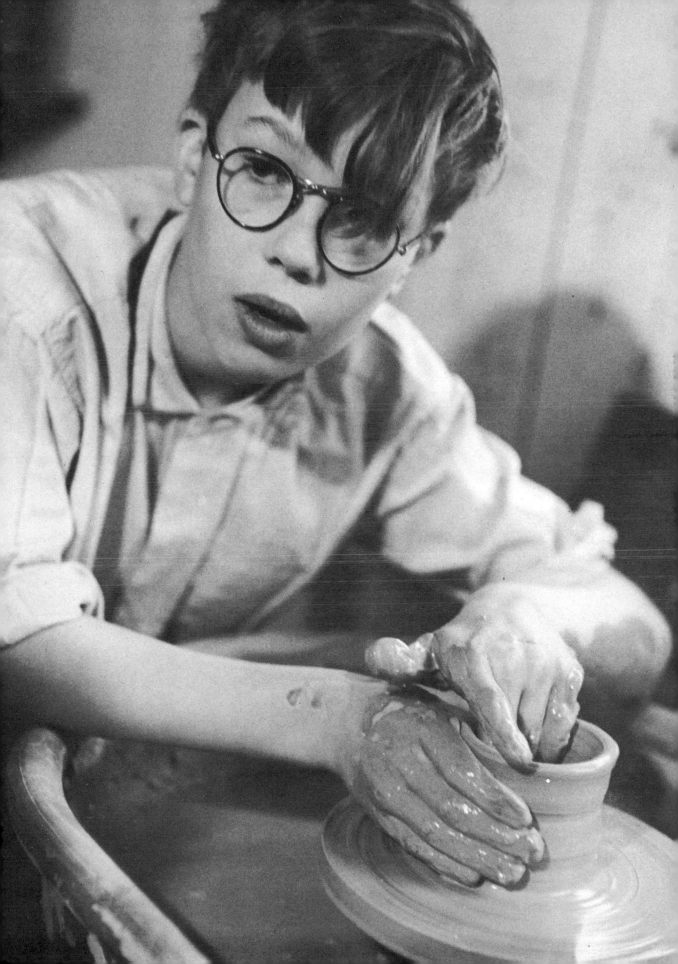

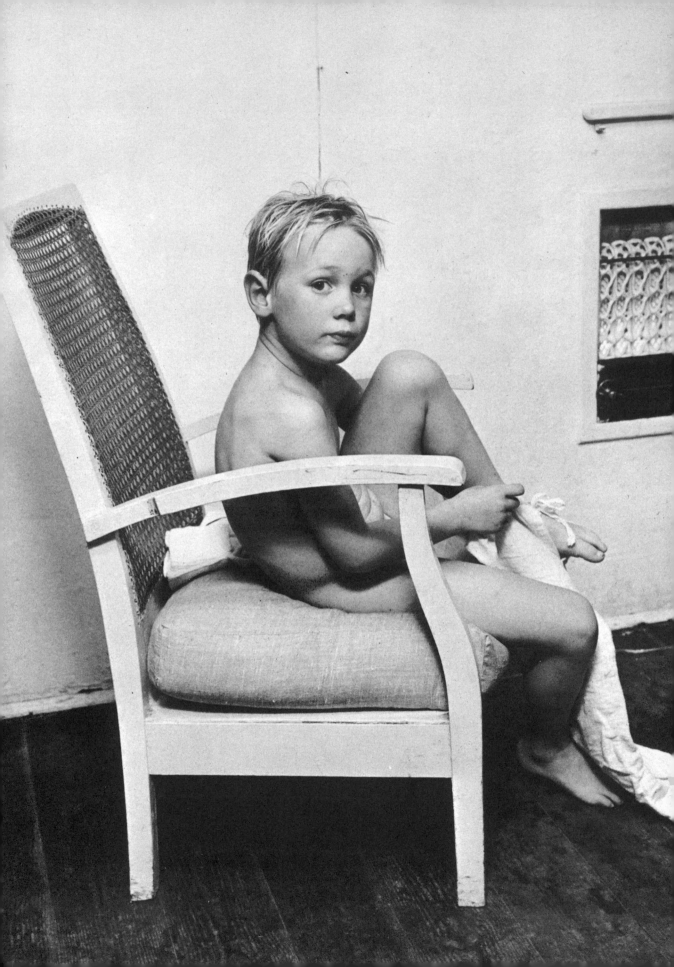

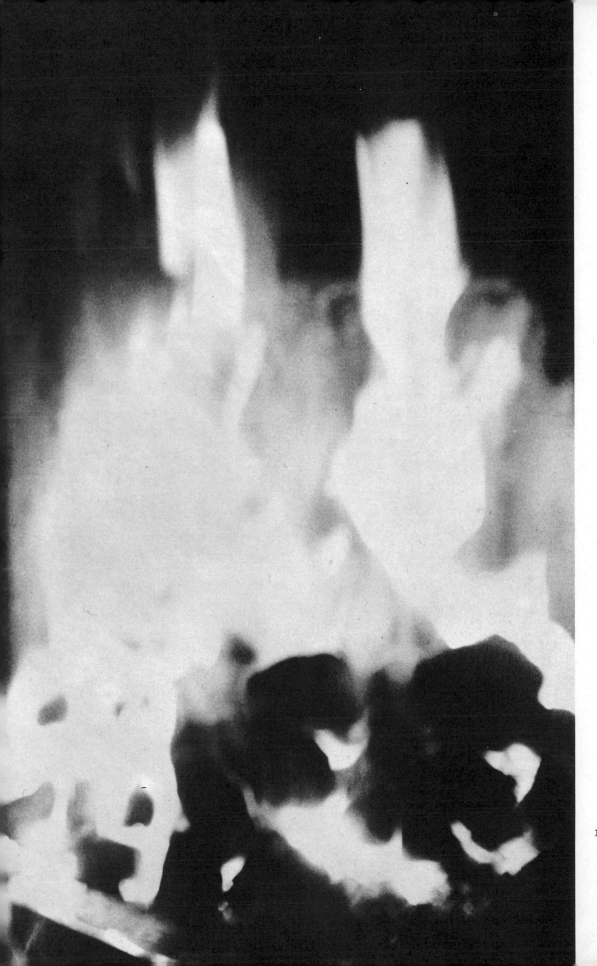

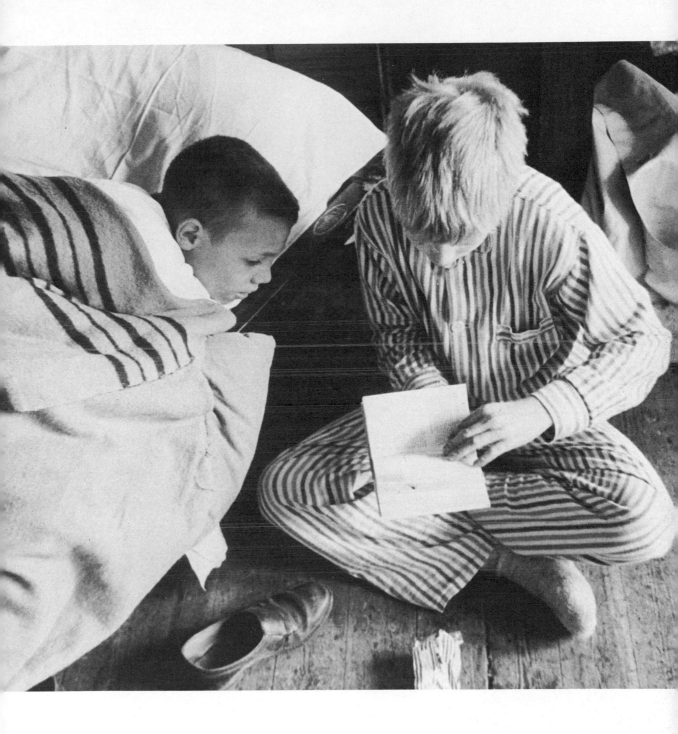

8. Saturday-Night General Meeting

SUMMERHILL is founded on freedom—freedom to do what you like as long as you don't interfere with someone else's freedom.

The big Saturday-night General Meeting (attended by every student and staff member along with housemothers, visitors, and anyone else who wishes to listen and join in) is led by one of the older students. Never the same student two weeks in a row.

The meeting is divided into three parts: Tribunal, Agenda, and Meeting. The Tribunal report is read first; it is a report from the day before when those students met who had a complaint to make or desired a fine imposed. You can appeal Tribunal. For example, if a child was fined money or anything on Friday, he or she could appeal this fine on Saturday night. The Agenda is given over to those students who have something important to say and who, during the week, have given their names to the secretary of the meeting. They are called on first. The meeting is then open to general discussion. It begins at 7:00 P.M. and usually runs until 8:30 P.M.

I attended ten General Meetings in my time at Summerhill, and the most dominating aspect of all was the vivid sense of fairness expressed by the children. Sometimes general rules were stiff or unusually severe, and within a week or two they were brought up again in the meeting, and usually changed. Most of the time I felt that what was dealt out was done for very constructive reasons, and here again it was rare when someone took it personally. It was not unusual to see someone accused of something, and that same person vote for the fine, whatever form it took. Each problem was discussed at length before proposals were made. Each side of the story was talked through. It was wonderful to see kids get up and say

things without fear in their eyes. It was wonderful to see a child of six or seven say something, and the entire community treat that child as an equal.

Through all these meetings Neill sat, usually saying very little or nothing at all. The same held true for the staff.

The children feel the school is theirs, and the running of it is their personal concern. For the most part, the older students hold it together, although at times the older members could do much more. Few of the older children had come all the way through Summerhill from the time they were five or six.

But with all the problems they faced, I have never seen a group of people handle themselves in such a mature and understanding way as these fifty-two children. Sure, there were problems they couldn't solve or deal with, but this was and is a living community where there was an effort made to correct injustices and unfairness, and in most cases they succeeded at least in bringing the problems into the open.

From these meetings and from all other aspects of Summerhill, these children are getting to know what it means to live with all sorts of people, with all sorts of individual problems. They learn to respect the other person's feelings and ideas, and most important, not to feel threatened by them. What they will take away from Summerhill is an inner security, looking at life as a beautiful thing, where the sun shines most of the time.

◄§ Complete Saturday-Night Meeting ୬►

CHAIRMAN: *Okay, everybody, quiet down! Tribunal. Carole, will you read it off?*

CAROLE: *Van versus Tim for going down the fire escape. One hour and a half of work for Tim in the garden.*
Judy versus Earl for breaking her door down. Earl fined sixpence and not allowed in her room.
Willard versus Julie for annoyance. Let off with a strong warning. Willard and Julie playing with fire again. No pocket money this week.
Ernie versus Nigel and Dave for chucking apples at him. They have to eat apples all day.

CHAIRMAN: *Right. Are there any appeals? Tim.*

TIM: *I want to appeal that fire-escape bit. I had no idea you weren't allowed on the fire escape.*

LARRY: *Hey, look at him, will you? Wow! Real sharp!*

CHAIRMAN: *Okay, quiet down, you two. You didn't know, Tim?*

TIM: *I didn't know, so do what you want. I'm telling you I didn't know the law.*

MILLIE: *Look, he knew, for it happened to Larry a few weeks ago, and Tim was here at the meeting. I think the fine should stick.*

CHAIRMAN: *All right, now look. If you want to talk, raise your hand. Okay? We'll vote on it. All in favor that Tim gets let off.*

NEILL: *For what? I can't hear; you people make so damn much noise.*

CHAIRMAN: *He was fined an hour and a half of work in the garden for going down the fire escape. All right. All in favor he is let off. All against. Sorry, mate, the fine sticks. Any more appeals? Right. First on the agenda. Larry.*

LARRY: *I wish that people who come down to the carriages would please keep the door closed when they go in or out. It's damn cold now, and I'd like everyone to remember this.*

CHAIRMAN: *Right. Will people please keep the carriage door closed when they go in or out. Clancy, you're next.*

CLANCY: *I'm fining Earl for going up to the balcony, but I don't want it to be a money fine.*

CHAIRMAN: *What do you want to do then, Clancy? You can't fine him now anyway.*

CLANCY: *I just want to give him a strong warning. That's all. I just want him to know in front of the community that he isn't allowed up in the balcony.*

CHAIRMAN: *Okay, Earl. Try not to go up in the balcony, will you, mate? The next time it may be more severe for you. Next on the agenda. Jerry.*

JERRY: *I'd like to bring up about the noise in first supper. There are about forty people acting like lunatics.*

CHAIRMAN: *What do you want, Jerry?*

JERRY: *I don't know. What powers do the dining-room officers have?*

CAROLE: *They have the power to chuck anyone who is disturbing supper, and those people have to eat in the sitting room.*

LARRY: *Can't Jerry eat in second supper instead?*

TIM: *Listen, mate, I want to eat in second supper too.*

CHAIRMAN: *Okay, now belt up, you. Raise your hand if you want to talk. Ena.*

ENA: *In regard to this, I would like to know if it is possible for the first dinner to be served through the hatch. It takes the servers a bloody great time to serve the other way, and the noise becomes appalling.*

EARL: *Ena, it's only a certain group who make noise.*

ENA: *And you're one of them, mate.*

[Laughter]

CHAIRMAN: *Look, let's take one thing at a time. All in favor that Jerry and Tom have the power to chuck anyone out of first supper who makes noise. Right. Against? Okay, carried. Now on to Ena's suggestion. All in favor that the little kids queue up for dinner.*

BRENDAN: *Hey, I don't think the older kids should vote, since they really have no say in this matter.*

CHAIRMAN: *Right. That's true. Just those that eat first dinner. All in favor. All against. Service will be through the hatch. Olly, you're next.*

OLLY: *Right. This is a request. I keep finding foreign bodies in the dirty linen closet. Now the only thing that goes in there is dirty linen. Not bits of wood or old trombones.*

[Laughter]

So will people just throw dirty linen there and nothing else? The second request is that on Thursday nights I borrow Peter's hut for what is known as a Sinatra session or an Ory orgy. Now, it makes me mad, when I am just getting with it, to have someone bang on the door. Now, I'm not going to let them in. Here I am in a trance, and someone starts banging. It's dangerous to my mental being.

[Laughter]

NEILL: *Mr. Chairman, will you have Olly or yourself explain who this chap Sinatra is?*

BRENDAN: *He's some hick singer, Neill.*

OLLY: *Watch it, mate.*

GWEN: *Don't be a nit, Neill.*

CHAIRMAN: *Right. You all heard what Olly said. Please try to comply with it. By the way, Agenda is over. Meeting open. Herb.*

HERB: *There was a Dominie book of Neill's on my photographic bag in the staff room, and now I assume that someone borrowed it, so whoever did borrow it, I would like to have it returned since it wasn't mine, and*   1 1 5 these books are hard to come by. It's called *A Dominie in Doubt* by A. S. Neill.

LARRY: *Hey, Mr. Chairman, who is A. S. Neill?*

[Laughter]

CHAIRMAN: *Okay, okay, pack it in now. Barbara.*

BARBARA: *I'd like to know which one of you crooks has my pen.*

SCOTT: *Hey, watch it there, mate.*

BARBARA: *I left it on the mantelpiece over the fireplace yesterday for about thirty seconds, and it's gone. It's a blue one.*

CLANCY: *Barbara, I found it. I have it in my room. I'll give it to you after the meeting.*

CHAIRMAN: *Right. Neill.*

NEILL: *Whenever I come out of my office in the afternoon, I walk down the hall, and I see lights burning when no one is in the rooms. Please put them out. It costs money. Another thing is, I'd like to know who the gentleman is—I assume it is a gentleman—who hasn't the strength to lift the lavatory seat.*

[Laughter]

I walk into the bogs, and the seat is all wet. Now, even the chairman has the strength to lift the seat.

CHAIRMAN: *Watch it, Neill.*

[Laughter]

Okay, okay. You all heard Neill. Please put out the lights, and lift the lavatory seat, you guys. Jerry.

JERRY: *I just remembered last week that I am the only one on the cutlery committee, and I'm lonesome.*

MILLIE: *What the hell is that?*

CHAIRMAN: *That is a committee that goes around making sure you blokes don't take forks and knives up to your rooms or use them for sculpting. If they see any cutlery, they can just take them without asking you. Okay, now, who wants to be on the committee with Jerry? There is room for only one. Don, do you want to say something?*

DON: *I want to know—um—a pen disappeared, and that fellow up there—if anyone finds it they should—it belongs to him.*

CHAIRMAN: *Don, old boy, that is another business.*

LARRY: *What the hell did he say, anyway?*

CLANCY: *I don't know, mate. He's only five, you know.*

CHAIRMAN: *Okay, let's get on with the vote. Bettie, Paul, Tom, and Alice want to be on the committee. All in favor of*

Bettie. Paul? Tom? Alice? Tom, you have it, old man.
Next business. Toro.

TORO: *I want to bring up Earl and Paul for hitting and bully-*
ing me all the time.

CHAIRMAN: *Do you want to fine them?*

TORO: *No, but I want something done.*

CHAIRMAN: *Right. Roy?*

ROY: *I propose that we put up a sign where those two blokes*
can't reach it that says "Earl and Paul love Toro."

EARL: *Hey!!*

TORO: *Hey, that's good. Ray for Roy.*

CHAIRMAN: *Okay, order, order here. That's enough now. Van.*

VAN: *Toro, I don't see where you have anything to complain*
about. You do the same thing all the time to every-
body else.

MILLIE: *Yeah, Toro, you do.*

CHAIRMAN: *Now look, Earl. Belt up, and don't say any more, or*
I'll chuck you out. Roy.

ROY: *Look, Toro brought Earl and Paul up. That's all. If*
Toro does the same thing, someone else bring him up.
There is no other business on the floor except Toro's
and the proposal.

CHAIRMAN: *Okay, all in favor that a sign be placed where they can't*
reach it that says, "Earl and Paul love Toro." Against.
Carried. Next business. Peter Wood.

WOOD: *I just want to say that no one is allowed out of Sum-*
merhill before twelve noon, if they are under fifteen.
That's not a Summerhill law but an English law set by
the government, so if you want to break laws, break
your own laws. It doesn't do any of us any good to be
seen downtown before twelve.

JOYCE: *That goes for Earl.*

EARL: *Look, you can tell Tim and Nigel and . . .*

WOOD: *Look, I'm telling everyone. You don't have to take it*
personally. I would just like all of you to stop it.

CAROLE: *Neill, isn't there a law that no one from Summerhill*
can go to the coffee bar? There are a few who have
been going down there.

NEILL: *Who are they?*

CAROLE: *Myrna and Emma and Scott and a few others.*

NEILL: *I had that place put off limits because there was a*
knifing there, and I don't want Summerhill people
brought into that kind of thing. There are a lot of

117

laborers around because of Sizwell, and they are getting drunk and breaking into shops, and I don't want anyone here getting into this kind of thing. This was a law I had to make to protect us all. I don't want the police down here telling me that one of you has been hurt. Just stay away from that place.

SCOTT: *I propose a two and sixpence fine for anyone caught down there.*

ROY: *Hey, Neill was going to fine me a quid.*

NEILL: *I can still do it, Roy.*

CHAIRMAN: *I'm going to take Scott's proposal. All in favor. All against. Carried. So watch it, will you? Ena.*

ENA: *I have heard over the past few weeks of distressed feelings about loaning little kids money and not being able to get it back.*

SEVERAL
VOICES: *Hear, hear!*

ENA: *There is a law that you aren't allowed to loan anyone money. Now would it be better to give out cinema money on cinema nights?*

SEVERAL
VOICES: *Oh, no. No, no.*

ENA: *Look, it is only a suggestion.*

CAROLE: *There is also a rule that if you loan money to kids under twelve, you do so at your own risk. If they don't pay you back, that's your hard luck.*

NEILL: *I propose that pocket money be given out on Monday.*

ROY: *Oh, hell, Neill.*

CHAIRMAN: *Look, belt up, all of you. Look, Neill, they want their pocket money on Saturday so they can have it for the fair, or else for sweets over the weekend. I don't think it is fair to take that away.*

NEILL: *Look, I don't care. It's your money. I just think it might give the little kids a chance to see the cinema once in a while.*

CHAIRMAN: *Look, Ena, can't you give out cinema money on Monday, and the rest of the money on the regular Saturday night?*

ENA: *No, it becomes too difficult for that. It's complicated enough without having to go through that as well.*

CHAIRMAN: *Let's drop it, then.*

ENA: *All right with me. I don't care.*

CHAIRMAN: *Libby, you want to say something?*

LIBBY: *I want to propose that if the cottage kids wake Scott*

118

or me up before first breakfast bell that they go to the back of the queue every morning that they do. They make a bloody great noise, and it's terrible for both of us.

CHAIRMAN: Right. Any discussion from the cottage kids? No? Right, then. All in favor that they go to the end of the queue each morning they wake Libby or Scott. Against. Carried. Any more business?

ENA: I have a request from Esther that people do not keep worrying her about their mail, and that they stay out of the kitchen during mealtime. If you have any mail it will be given to you at break or at dinner or at tea. Don't keep bothering the kitchen people. They have a job to do without having to argue with you all the time.

CHAIRMAN: Right. Anyone else? Bob.

BOB: I have dropped a number of magazines and books in the sitting rooms, and I suggest that when you are finished with them, you put them back on the table and not take them to your rooms. They are for everyone.

CHAIRMAN: Okay, will everyone please keep this in mind? Any more business? Right. Meeting closed.

⋖§ General Meeting II §⋗

CHAIRMAN: Can we have some order here, please? All right, now, order. Will you shut the door please, Wood? First business on the agenda.

ROY: Hey, what about the Tribunal report?

CHAIRMAN: Oh, right. Roz, will you read Tribunal? Sorry, old man.

ROZ: Paul versus Earl for throwing matches at him. Earl fined sixpence. Alice versus Julie for chucking raisins around. Julie doesn't get any raisins next week.
Earl versus Don for playing with fire. Don lights the bonfire on Monday.
Emile versus Mort for hitting him at supper. Mort to eat supper last all week.
Lou versus Ben for putting shoe polish on his trunk. Dropped with a strong warning.

CHAIRMAN: Right. Now, is there anyone who wants to make an appeal? Earl?

121

EARL: *I think I was fined too much.*

CHAIRMAN: *State your case.*

EARL: *I didn't intentionally throw the matches at him, and besides, they weren't lit.*

CHAIRMAN: *That's beside the point, Earl. Lit or not, it's a stupid thing to do.*

EARL: *I didn't see him there anyway.*

CHAIRMAN: *It's still a stupid thing to throw matches anyway.*

PAUL: *He damn well saw me, and threw them at me.*

EARL: *I did not.*

CHAIRMAN: *No cross talk now. How much was he fined?*

ROZ: *Sixpence.*

CHAIRMAN: *Well, that isn't so much.*

EARL: *For me it is.*

CHAIRMAN: *How much do you think you should be fined?*

EARL: *Threepence.*

NEILL: *What was he fined for? I can't hear if you speak so damn low.*

CHAIRMAN: *He was fined sixpence for flinging matches at Paul, and now he wants it lowered to threepence. All right. All in favor that Earl is fined threepence instead of sixpence. All against. You're still fined sixpence.*

EARL: *Oh, hell!*

CHAIRMAN: *Anybody else want to appeal? Right, first business on the agenda. Olly.*

OLLY: *I'm not charging anyone, but someone very kindly borrowed my bike last week, smashed the pedal up, and just put it back in the garage. I had to go to the expense to get it mended, but I think it is a pretty poor excuse and attitude that somebody borrows something without permission—breaks it—and then just sticks it back. It cost me about ten bob to have it mended, and I find it rather unpleasant. First of all, my poor old bike can't stand it. It's quite old, and that's why I don't lend it to people. I don't particularly care who did it now. I just think that if people are going to borrow something, they should at least ask permission first.*

EARL: *I think it was Joyce.*

OLLY: *Look, Mate, I'm not interested in who it was at this point. I just want it stopped.*

CHAIRMAN: *Is that all, Olly?*

OLLY: *Yes.*

CHAIRMAN: *Right. Next business on the agenda. Gwen.*

GWEN: *I want to know who and how I am going to be repaid for the damage done by Phyllis the other night when she broke the windows and broke my things as well. Things have just gone too far.*

CHAIRMAN: *What was broken?*

GWEN: *Two bottles of my medicine, a mirror, a gold watch chain, a gramophone box, and an antique box.*

NEILL: *Mr. Chairman, will you kindly have her speak up? I'm not as keen in my hearing as I used to be.*

CHAIRMAN: *She wants to know who will pay for the damage Phyllis did last night. Did you know that she broke up a lot of things, Neill?*

NEILL: *No, I was away lecturing, and I just got back about two hours ago.*

CHAIRMAN: *Well, she did this last night, and now Gwen wants to know who will pay her for these things. Look, will you all be quiet? If you don't want a meeting, we won't have it. Ena, will this be put on her bill?*

ENA: *Yes, it will.*

CHAIRMAN: *It will? Right. Okay, Gwen? You see Ena about this. Next business on the agenda. Scott.*

SCOTT: *I'm bringing up Larry again for smashing my door in again. Only this time it came down and smashed my bookcase as well, and I want to know if it is going to be fixed. I'm getting a little tired of my door coming down once a week or so.*

[Laughter]

It isn't funny.

CHAIRMAN: *Order here. The next person talking will be fined.*

LARRY: *I didn't break his door.*

SCOTT: *I don't know what you'd call it, but I just saw my door coming into my room and you on top of it.*

CHAIRMAN: *Okay, what are we going to do about the door?*

OLLY: *I thought we had settled this last night.*

LARRY: *I think he likes his door broken. It gives him a chance to go around the school telling people about it.*

CHAIRMAN: *Order. Will you people stop mucking about.*

SCOTT: *I come in at night, and there is no door. I'm not complaining. I just want my door.*

[Laughter]

CHAIRMAN: *Neill?*

NEILL: *It is all very good to laugh at this, but we seem to have an epidemic of people breaking doors. Peter and Harry*

123

have to go and mend these things, and now why should we have to do this for you? I think we shall call in Parish next door—have him mend it, and send the bill to the guys who broke the door.

OLLY: *That's what we arranged, Neill.*

NEILL: *Then why isn't it carried out? Did Larry break the door? Yes.*

CHAIRMAN: *Well, that's it, then. Look, Nigel and Lou, will you pack it up or get out? If you're going to have one of your bloody fights, do it in the sitting room. Earl.*

EARL: *I'd like to bring Julie up for coming in at all hours, slamming doors, and waking everyone.*

NIGEL: *Look, Earl, if you weren't up yourself at that hour you wouldn't hear him.*

EARL: *I don't want to fine anybody for this. I just want him to be a bit more quiet when he comes in. Just sort of like take his shoes off. And another thing, Nigel, almost every night this week I have been in bed before eleven, and that's a miracle for me.*

ROGER: *Look, Julie, all they're asking is that you be quiet about it.*

JULIE: *I am quiet.*

ROGER: *Then be a little bit more quiet. That's all, mate.*

CHAIRMAN: *Look, damn it, you two. Pack it in. Wood.*

WOOD: *I'd just like to remind everyone in this meeting that the chairman has the right to fine anyone he or she wishes, if they are disturbing the meeting.*

CHAIRMAN: *Right. Next business on the agenda. None? Meeting open. Wood.*

WOOD: *I have requested a few times that you do not bathe after four-thirty or before seven in the evening, because the boiler won't stand it. I repeat the request again for the benefit of those idiots that have forgotten.*

[Laughter]

It's not really funny, and you all know it.

NEILL: *I know this is something we have talked about, but I feel I have to bring it up again, and that is bedtimes. You kids are running around this house at all hours, and as I said before, it's becoming a health problem, not a government problem.*

GWEN: *I think it's working better, Neill. Before, we stayed up for a great number of hours. Now we don't.*

MYRNA: *Oh, what the hell. There have been riots all week. What do you mean, it's working?*

ULLA: *This is a bit absurd. Last night there was such a row in the house, it was terrible.*

CHAIRMAN: *Look, I've had enough. One more outburst like that, and I'll close this meeting. Neill, do you have any ideas?*

NEILL: *No, my concern is the health of the children. If you can't keep the laws you make, then the staff will decide about bedtimes, and then we'll make it a strict school. Is that what you want? I just can't afford to have kids get sick. The school can be closed for that.*

CHAIRMAN: *Neill, how are you giving out pocket money? This meeting is being closed. I won't stand for this noise.*

NEILL: *I'll give it out by nationality. All the Scottish people first and—*

[Laughter]

—No, no. I'll give it out according to size. Little ones first.

CHAIRMAN: *Okay. Meeting closed.*

⋞ General Meeting III ⋟

(No Tribunal—left out)

CHAIRMAN: *First business on the agenda. Bob.*

BOB: *I have two things I want to make known. One, some-body borrowed my work gloves about ten days ago, and they haven't returned them. I would like to have them back.*

CLANCY: *I have them, Bob. I'll give them to you at the end of the meeting. Sorry about that.*

BOB: *Okay. The other thing is this. Since last Saturday, just for kicks, I started keeping track of how many times I was asked for money, and between last Saturday and Thursday, when people caught on to what I was doing, I was asked eighty-seven times*

[Laughter]

by thirty-two different people. I'm not counting staff, and if I had said "yes" to all requests I would have given out twelve pounds, fourteen and four, which is twice as much as what a teacher makes here in a week, and half the time I said "no," I was called stingy. I know it's funny, looking back on it, but living with it from day to day makes life rather unpleasant.

ENA: *We've been living with that for twenty years, Bob.*

CHAIRMAN: *Right, so if you don't want to be put down in Bob's book, don't ask him for money. Next business.*

MYRNA: *I'd like to say something about this lost-and-found business, and the rewards. I think this reward business should be stopped. Certain people this week have been taking advantage of this. They have stolen things, and have waited until a reward has gone up, and then they queue up for the reward for finding something they stole in the first place. I'd like to propose that no re-wards be given for things found. I just think it en-courages people to steal things. We should be honest*

127

enough with each other so that if we find anything, we should give it to Carole to post on the board, and not wait until a reward is put up.

BRENDAN: Look, that's up to the person who wants to give a reward, isn't it?

MYRNA: Well, I think the community has a perfect right to decide what it is worth.

CAROLE: Look, Myrna, you may lose something that isn't worth threepence, but may be worth a great deal more in how you feel about it. Why should the community decide how you feel about it?

MYRNA: Look, all I'm saying is that people cannot put up a reward without bringing it to the attention of the community. If you lose something, you have to make an announcement before the community before a reward can be posted. Okay?

CHAIRMAN: All right, all in favor of that. All against. It isn't carried.

ROY: Take another vote.

WILF: I don't think a vote is necessary. All Myrna is doing is appealing to the community not to bring up a reward straight away. That's all.

CHAIRMAN: Okay. Is that okay with you, Myrna?

MYRNA: Yes.

CHAIRMAN: Right.

CAROLE: You must remember that sometimes it is a good thing. Remember that time that woman lost her keys in the hockey field. She offered a reward, and they were found in about two hours.

LES: I propose this meeting is closed.

WILF: Now, wait a minute. I think this is an important matter that Myrna has brought up. I think that what she says is quite true—that rewards do encourage people to steal, and it should be dealt with here and now.

CAROLE: I think this is a bit much. There have been things that have been genuinely lost, and people put up a reward because they know that everyone keeps their eyes open.

SCOTT: Look, Myrna. I don't think you have to propose this. It is a personal thing between the person who lost the article or whatever and what he wants to do about it. Look, I don't think we have a right to say that someone cannot give a reward when he or she wants to. Nobody has the right to say that. It's your life.

WILF: I'd just like to reply to Carole here. She is right. People

<dd>shouldn't be stopped from offering rewards when they want to. It is a suggestion that before this is done, you appeal to the community. No one said you had to do this. You can do what you want.</dd>

MYRNA: *I think the community should decide when a reward is necessary.*

BRENDAN: *Hell, no! If I decide I want to put up a reward, that's my business—not yours.*

CHAIRMAN: *Okay, okay. That's enough now. I think we've talked this subject dead. Anyone else? Neill.*

NEILL: *I want to say something quite serious, and I don't want any laughter about it. I made a law at the beginning of this term about smoking if you are under sixteen. I made this law because the government told all schools to discourage smoking among children, and Summerhill can't stand out against the whole of the schools of England. I had to follow on, and make a law that you can't smoke under sixteen. Now, a lot of people are smoking under sixteen, and quite openly. Well, I'm telling you now, but before I say it, some of you think I'm an old softie. Neill is an easygoing guy. Well, I'm going to tell you all something. You have to choose whether you are going to smoke here or not. If you're going to smoke here, you're not coming back. I'm telling Clancy's parents that. I'm telling others that as well. I've got to carry this law through. I can't punish you. Only the community can punish, but I can say, all right, if you don't want to live the Summerhill way, you're not coming back. You can call this a punishment if you like. And that applies to the Americans too. I'm going to have this law carried out for my own safety and for yours as well. So don't feel you can come here, and do as you like. You can't.*

CHAIRMAN: *Right. We've all heard Neill. You take it from there. Is there any more business? Meeting closed, then.*

9. Acting

Every Sunday evening after supper, Neill holds his acting class. It has always been one of Neill's beliefs that children never get enough of fantasy play—never get enough of acting out what they feel.

The class is usually made up of the younger kids with a few of the older ones around. Neill presents a situation, the barest of outlines, and the kids take over from there.

Here again, the children perform openly and freely, without fear of being laughed at, and when there has been a particularly original performance, the children clap long and loud.

NEILL:: *Now, here is a story I want you to act out. You are a burglar trying to crack a safe, and while you're doing it, I'm the owner of the house, and I come on the scene and speak to you. I want to see you react. Now think about it before raising your hands. Okay, you first.*

LOU: *Where's the safe, Neill?*

NEILL: *In the middle of the room. Go on, now.*
  (Lou works on the safe.)
  You're not very good, are you? Why don't you learn your trade?

LOU: *Oh, it's you. (Continues working on the safe.)*

NEILL: *Now, look. Would you continue working on the safe after the man of the house finds you?*

LOU: *But I know you, Neill.*

NEILL: *I know, but you're not acting, lad. Oh, God! Someone*

1 3 1

else try acting now. I'm not Neill. I'm the owner of the house, you chumps.
(An older boy starts working on the safe.)
Not bad. Oh, stop it, man. You're a bungler. I can open . . .

BRENDAN: *Look, mate, I'm trying to open this safe, so will you belt up?*

NEILL: *Do you know who I am?*

BRENDAN: *Look, mate, belt up. Two thieves can't crack a safe at the same time.*

NEILL: *Oh, I see. That's rather good, but that happens to be my safe.*

BRENDAN: *Oh, really? (Smiling very weakly.)*

NEILL: *That's right.*
(Brendan jumps out the window.)
Okay, next. (Pause.) Not bad, not bad, but this is my house.

CLANCY: *Stand aside while I go on with my work, will you, Bud?*

NEILL *(Picking up imaginary telephone): Police? This is Sir John Brown, 64 Lindale Gardens. There's a burglar in my house.*

CLANCY: *Who me, a burglar?*

NEILL: *Who are you, then?*

CLANCY: *I'm a crack safer. I mean a safecracker.*

NEILL: *Oh, I see. Excuse me, officer, he's a crack safer, not a burglar. Okay, good. Now stand over there and crack up. Next.*
Hey, what are you doing in my house?

SCOTT: *Okay, stick 'em up. Come on, move over. Now, open that safe.*

NEILL: *Good, good. The only one to think of that. He's all right. Make a fine burglar once he leaves Summerhill. Okay, anyone else? Go on, Myrna, have a go. Rather unusual profession for a lady, isn't it?*

MYRNA: *You! It's no good, you're not going to stop me now. I've been looking for this for years.*

NEILL: *For what?*

MYRNA: *You can call the police if you like. I'll plead insanity.*

NEILL: *Well, go on. I'll plead insanity too, and they'll can us both. Okay. Next.*
(A little girl of eight.)
You're not very good at your job, are you?

LISA: *Oh, good evening.*

NEILL: Good evening. What are you doing in my house near my safe?

LISA: Well, you see, I'm a safe inspector. I'm just inspecting your safe.

NEILL: Oh? Don't you think it would be a good idea for you to ring the bell, and come in through the front door?

LISA: Well, no, sir. You see, we're trying to see people's reactions to burglars, so I dressed up as a burglar to see how you'd take it.

NEILL: Well, very nice. Is the safe all right? '

LISA: Yes, quite. Well, goodbye.

NEILL: Before you go, do you mind emptying your pockets?

LISA: Oh, ha ha, yes, of course.

NEILL: The other one, now. There is still a fiver in there.

LISA: Oh, yes, how foolish. Well, goodbye.

NEILL: Goodbye. Now, that was wonderful.

NEILL: I've advertised for a film star, and I want people to come up one by one and apply for the job. Okay? Right.

SCOTT: Hello there, Mr. Goldie.

NEILL: You've got real Holly— What's the name of that place, now?

SCOTT: Hollywood. You know, Mr. Goldie.

NEILL: Oh, yes, you've got a real Hollywood smile.

SCOTT: Yeah, yeah, sure do, yeah, yeah.

NEILL: Your teeth your own?

SCOTT: Yeah, yeah. I got them from the best company in the world, yeah.

NEILL: Well, the scene is a place in England called Oxford. Do you speak Oxfordish?

SCOTT: Huh? Oxfordish? What the hell. Oh, yeah, yeah, sure I do, yeah.

NEILL: All right. Stand over there and put it on.

SCOTT: How do you want me to put it on?

NEILL: Oh, any way it fits.

SCOTT: I dare say, that is rather ruddy well nice of you. Just top drawer and smashing. How was I, sir? Do I get the part? Yessir, Hollywood, my home town, yeah. Am I hired? I can sing too, yeah.

NEILL: Okay, okay, just get over there.

MARTY: Uh—hullo there, Mr. Goldstein.

NEILL: The name is Mr. Goldwyn.

MARTY: Oh, yeah? Well—uh—I read that you needed a film star, and here I is. I mean, am. What do you say, do I do?

NEILL: Do you do what?

MARTY: I mean—uh—do I get the part? I want to be one of your movie stars. Like I mean, I can sing and dance, and, well, you know, man, I—uh—well, you know, man, I sing like.

NEILL: Like what?

MARTY: No, no, man, you ain't with it. I mean like, wow!

NEILL: Okay, okay, stand over there and make a noise like a carrot. Okay, next.

TOM: Hi there, Sammy baby. I'd like to have a part in your new film, baby. I really would, you darling fellow. What do you say, Sammy baby?

NEILL: What kind of part?

TOM: I'd like to play Superman, baby.

NEILL: Do you know that Superman doesn't eat soup?

TOM: That's all right, Sammy baby. If it's like Ena's soup, that's cool. How about the part, baby?

NEILL: Well, stand over there, baby, and I'll let you know.

TOM: Hey, where's the movie star's stand?

NIGEL: Up your ass.

TOM: Hey, Sammy baby, where's up your ass?

NEILL: Okay, okay, right over by the tree. Okay, next. You.

GWEN: Hello there, I'm here to sign the contract.

NEILL: The contract?

GWEN: Yes, the contract for the movie you are letting me star in.

NEILL: I am?

GWEN: Of course, you nit. I'm here to sign, and I'm a busy girl, so let's not fool around.

NEILL: Well, I don't know. Can you act?

GWEN: Well, I never. Can I act? I've been acting all my life.

NEILL: I know that, but can you act in a play?

GWEN: Listen, Mr. Producer or whatever. I have never been so insulted. Just for that you can keep your old contract. Say, do you have carfare for me?

NEILL: Okay, that was good. You try it.

JOYCE: Oh, Mr. Goldwyn, my love, my one and only, my lover. Please give me the part. (She rushes into Neill's arms.) Oh, I can't live without you. Oh, Mr. Goldwyn, you're wonderful, you're beautiful, I love you madly.

ROY: Hey, Neill, you're turning color.

NEILL: Okay, okay, ha ha. That's fine. Very nice.

LOU: Hey, Neill, what are you blushing for?

NEILL: I'm St. Peter at the Golden Gate, and you're all trying to get into heaven. You've all died, ha ha, and you've come up from hell, and I want to see how you approach me. Well, come on. Don't any of you want to go to heaven? You try it.

SCOTT: Hello. Are you St. Peter?

NEILL: Yes, yes. I think so.

SCOTT: Well—um—I'm trying to get into heaven. Which way is it?

NEILL: It doesn't make any difference. What sort of person are you?

SCOTT: Well, I'm a fabulous person actually. I've only told around a thousand lies, and I've only killed a few people.

NEILL: You expect to go to heaven after all that?

SCOTT: Of course, why not?

NEILL: Well, that's rather original. Maybe you'll help some of them in here. Okay, this way.

MC PHAIL (A former Summerhillian visiting the school): Okay, Neill, I'll try it, only I'm coming from heaven. Pardon me, but are you St. Peter of the administrative department?

NEILL: Yes, I am.

MC PHAIL: Well, I have a complaint to make. Those dammed 707's keep moving my cloud about, and it's disgusting.

NEILL: Oh, I see. Excuse me, but who are you?

MC PHAIL: Well, I came via a shortcut, actually.

NEILL: What rank do you have?

MC PHAIL: Well, actually, I'm making sure I like it before going in.

NEILL: You can't do that. How did you pass me before?

MC PHAIL: Well, you see I have a mate, and he owes me some money down below and . . .

NEILL: Oh, I see. Well, off to hell with you. Okay, next. Hey you, don't get so close. You're not a homo, are you?

TOM: No, I'm not a homo. I'm just looking at you.

NEILL: Oh, good!

TOM: Say, who are you?

NEILL: Stand over there, will you?

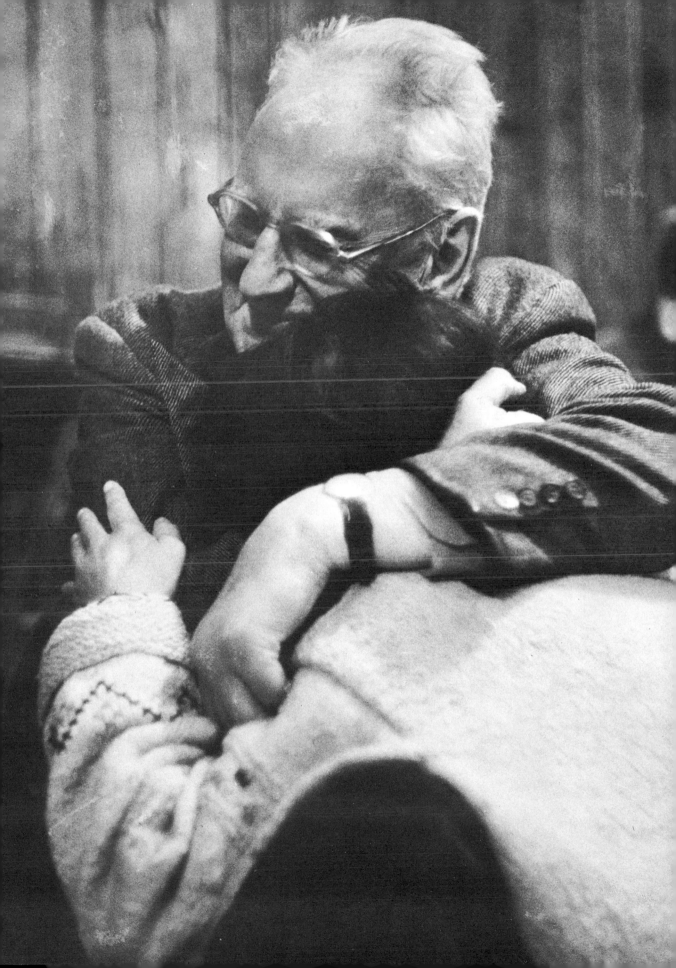

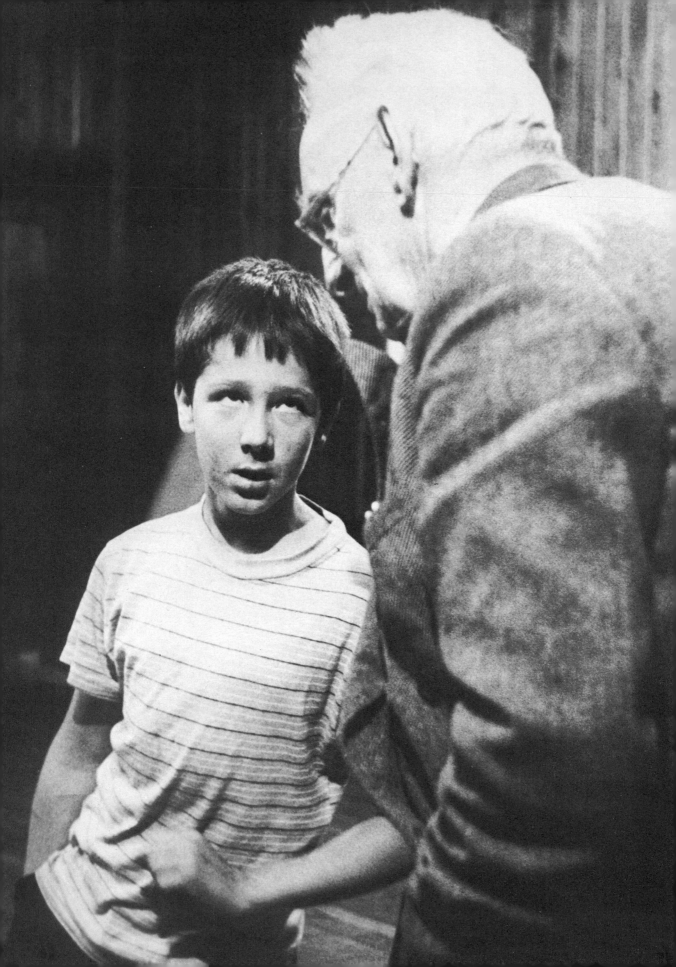

TOM: Hey, you watch who you're talking to that way, mate.

NEILL: What are you doing here?

TOM: I want to know who you are, mate.

NEILL: My name is Peter.

TOM: Say, that's a nice homey name.

NEILL: You can call me Pete for short.

TOM: You remind me of a guy who . . .

NEILL: Never mind the guy. Do you want to get into heaven or not?

TOM: Oh, no! I don't believe in heaven. I'm an atheist.

NEILL: Oh-ho! An atheist, are you?

TOM: That's right, mate.

NEILL: Well, there are a lot of atheists in hell.

TOM: Well, I don't believe in that either, mate, so I'll stay right here.

NEILL: Okay, goodbye. Go on, you damn atheist you.

TOM: Boy what a nut he is. Pete for short.

ROY: Hey, bud, how much are the tickets?

NEILL: How much you have on you?

ROY: Oh, not much. About four quid.

NEILL: Okay, give me half.

ROY: Righto, mate, see you.

NEILL: Hey! Don't tell anybody, will you?
Okay, you be the last.

CLANCY: (Comes upon Neill, snapping a camera): Say, could you tell me about your second divorce? You are St. Peter, aren't you? Well, good. Now, I'm from the Daily Blab, and our paper wants to do a feature on you. Now could you tell us a little about yourself?

NEILL: No. I'm not a very big guy. I only keep this golden key.

CLANCY: How much is it worth?

NEILL: You've been educated in America, I see.

CLANCY: Obviously. Can I see the key?

NEILL: Oh, no! I never give it up.

CLANCY: Well, then, a picture.

NEILL: Get out of here. I don't want you here.

CLANCY: Well, if that's your attitude, keep your old clouds.

NEILL: Okay. Now I'm going to be a governor of a prison. You've had a few years in prison, and so when you are set free you have to go to the governor's office, and he talks to you before you leave. Now, who will be the first criminal?

139

Come in. Well, you're finally getting out.

NIGEL: Yessir.

NEILL: How many years were you here?

NIGEL: Forty-five.

NEILL: Forty-five years? What did you do?

NIGEL: I killed my wife.

NEILL: What are you going to do when you leave?

NIGEL: Kill another wife.

NEILL: Okay, out you go. Now look, that wasn't real. That was bad acting. You don't get forty-five years for killing your wife. I want better acting. You try it. Hello, Smith.

JERRY: Hello, sir.

NEILL: What was your number again?

JERRY: Three, seven, zero, five, one.

NEILL: Oh, yes, well, what exchange was . . .

JERRY: Hey, Neill, that was pretty bad.

NEILL: Okay, okay. So you are going out into the wide world. What were you in for?

JERRY: Robbery with violence.

NEILL: Well, you've been a well-behaved prisoner. Have you enjoyed it?

JERRY: Can't say that I have.

NEILL: What's your trade?

JERRY: I'm a builder.

NEILL: Oh, I see.

JERRY: That's how I was able to build that ladder I tried to escape with a few months back.

NEILL: Oh, I see. I remember you now.

JERRY: It didn't work.

NEILL: Obviously. I hope you go straight, Smith. Got a wife?

JERRY: No, a girl friend.

NEILL: Oh, I see. Any children?

JERRY: No, sir.

NEILL: Well, goodbye, Smith.

JERRY: Goodbye.

NEILL: That was fine. Anybody else?

BRENDAN: I'm leaving.

NEILL: You're what?

BRENDAN: I'm leaving.

NEILL: Why?

BRENDAN: Because my sentence is over.

NEILL: Was it a grammatical sentence?

BRENDAN: Oh, brother, Neill is at it again.

ROY: *Pack it in, Neill.*

BRENDAN: *You know what I went in for?*

NEILL: *No.*

BRENDAN: *Shooting a governor.*

NEILL: *Oh, I see. Did you kill him?*

BRENDAN: *No, just shot him. He told a joke.*

NEILL: *Well, you haven't got a gat on you now, have you?*

BRENDAN: *I'm not saying.*

NEILL: *Okay, good. Next.*

LOU: *Listen, Governor, I'm leaving, and you're not stopping me.*

NEILL: *Why should I?*

LOU: *That's right, so move it, mate. You want to know what I'm here for?*

NEILL: *Pinching milk bottles?*

LOU: *Wrong.*

NEILL: *What, then?*

LOU: *I went downtown before twelve.*

NEILL: *Oh, well, good. Very nicely done.*

NEILL: *We'll have an old one now. Two people are talking, and one is trying to provoke the other, and the other doesn't want to be provoked. Try it.*

PHIL: *Right, but I mean Americans are absolutely disgusting. Now, let's face it. It's true, isn't it?*

TOM: *Well—um—I guess you're right.*

PHIL: *Of course I'm right. Another thing I don't like about American people: when you're talking to them, they just carry on.*

TOM: *Well—um—yes, well, I suppose you re right.*

PHIL: *Right, that's what I'm trying to tell you about the American people. Look at Cuba. I mean those poor Russians. All they were trying to do was help Cuba. I mean, after all, the Russians are pretty short of cigars.*

TOM: *Well, yes, I really think you're right.*

PHIL: *So they gave them some rockets. America just blew its top over nothing. I mean, it just shows you that the American people have no control over their emotions whatsoever. Right?*

TOM: *By the way, what nationality are you anyway?*

PHIL: *Nationality? Well—um—Chinese actually. Ming So Ching Chow.*

NEILL: *Good, good. Okay. That's it for tonight.* 141

Acknowledgments

I should like to acknowledge the help and advice given me by Len Silverman, and the Nikon Camera Company, for the additional photographic equipment needed in completing this project.

I should also like to thank Anne and Peter Piper, of London, England, for their graciousness and selflessness in making their home my home.